PAINT CAN!

Children's Rooms

Patterns & Projects for Colorful, Creative Spaces

Sunny Goode

photographs by Kip Dawkins

STERLING

New York / London
www.sterlingpublishing.com

A Lark Production
3 West Main Street #103
Irvington, NY 10533

Library of Congress Cataloging-in-Publication Data

Goode, Sunny.
    Paint can! children's rooms : patterns & projects for colorful, creative spaces /
Sunny Goode ; photographs by Kip Dawkins.
          p. cm.
      "A Lark Production."
      Includes index.
      ISBN-13: 978-1-4027-4512-6
        1. House painting--Amateurs' manuals. 2. Texture painting--Amateurs'
manuals. 3. Interior decoration--Amateurs' manuals. 4. Children's rooms. I.
Title. II. Title: Children's rooms, patterns & projects for colorful, creative spaces.

    TT323.G554 2008
    698'.14--dc22

                                       2007052521

10 9 8 7 6 5 4 3 2 1

Published by Sterling Publishing Co., Inc.
387 Park Avenue South, New York, NY 10016
© 2008 by Sunny Goode
Distributed in Canada by Sterling Publishing
c/o Canadian Manda Group, 165 Dufferin Street
Toronto, Ontario, Canada M6K 3H6
Distributed in the United Kingdom by GMC Distribution Services
Castle Place, 166 High Street, Lewes, East Sussex, England BN7 1XU
Distributed in Australia by Capricorn Link (Australia) Pty. Ltd.
P.O. Box 704, Windsor, NSW 2756, Australia

Book design and layout: Susan Fazekas

Printed in China

Sterling ISBN 978-1-4027-4512-6

For information about custom editions, special sales, premium and
corporate purchases, please contact Sterling Special Sales
Department at 800-805-5489 or specialsales@sterlingpublishing.com.

For Presley, Whit, Beck & Clarkie

acknowledgments

I'M GRATEFUL TO Lisa DiMona and Flynn Berry for making a second book happen as fast as the first; to Isabel Stein for keeping all the details straight; and to Anne Barthel and Myrsini Stephanides for the opportunity.

Thanks to Lucy for being a great team player and for help putting all of this together to share.

To Kip for your amazing visual talent, patience, and humor.

To Read, thanks for continuing to see our vision. You are the best!

To Pres, Whit, and Beck—you are always my inspiration. I love you so much!

Special thanks to Mom and Dad and many friends, who continue to make me laugh during this process.

Heartfelt thanks to all of my clients, who so graciously opened their homes to be photographed for this book: the Ackerlys, Boggs, Siewers, Hunters, Fitzgeralds, Smiths, Coles, and Cockrells. Your willingness to share cool ideas made it a lot more fun!

contents

part **1**

about
paint

part **2**

newborn through age 3
nurseries
for wee ones

part **3**

ages 4 through 8
rooms to play and grow in

part **4**

ages 9 through 12
rooms to think and dream in

let the good times roll

I HAVE ALWAYS BEEN DRAWN TO COLOR. In my own house, I love opening my green front door and walking into a hot pink entry-way. The world outside can be dull, so entering a jewel-box of a house is a wonderful way to come home. Color draws emotions out of us: What's more cheerful than a sunshine-yellow kitchen or more soothing than a pale blue bedroom? Harness the power of colors, and you'll want to spend more time puttering around your house.

I've painted over the walls in my house so many times that if you were to cut through to the original surface, it would look like a cross-section of the fossil record: there is the deep red era, and then the turquoise stage. I am equally passionate about my clients' houses. I became a decorative painter to help people learn to use color to enrich their environment. My company, Sunny's Goodtime Paints, helps people mix and match textures and colors to create the particular look they want: an old stone wall, a wash of color, modern tone-on-tone, a layer of glazes, a warm fresco plaster.

A colorful clown toy and a bedspread were the color inspirations for the freehand loops and balloons painted as a border in this room. For paint details, see the Loop-de-Loop project (page 59).

Cotton candy stripes, with color inspired by the fabrics in the room, enliven a girl's room and contrast with the green bed frame. For paint details, see the Cotton Candy Stripes project (page 95).

In my first book, *Paint Can!*, I shared my ideas on how anyone can use decorative painting to make their home feel just right for them. This book explores how decorative painting can work for children's rooms. Children are sensitive to their environments, so the changes in color you'll find in this book can have a big impact. I will show you how to wrap your daughter's room in bands of color or paint your son's nursery with marching elephants, creating a space that's all their own. You can give your child a room of color and lightness, a bright, safe space where they are free to grow and explore. In times past, a new child spurred people to get together and sew a quilt or create some other handmade treasure for the newcomer. Think of painting as your own form of barn raising. Welcome your child to the world!

Each child is different. And her room should be as individual as her name—a space to escape to where she can feel completely at ease. A good friend once told me to pay attention to what a child is drawn to from toddlerhood to around age five: "This," she said, "is what they will be drawn to when they are older." Since it is easy to forget what a child likes at age three, write it down so you remember! Create rooms that encourage their interests—nature, sports, art, dance. When creating children's spaces, you also need to be able to laugh with them, to let go and be creative with them! I wanted my son to model his rugby shirt for our photo of the Rugby Stripe room, for example, but no manner of coaxing would get him to do it. Like I said, you just have to laugh. So use the ideas in this book to have fun and to create rooms your kids will love!

A room for a child who loves fishing was inspired by the colors of this wooden fish buoy. For paint details, see the Gone Fishin' project (page 71).

A monogram adds detail.

PAINTING FOR CHILDREN

I love creating spaces for little people. When I was expecting my first child, I knew almost immediately what I wanted for the walls in the nursery: a light periwinkle wash with a big, whimsical curlicue border in preppy green. I would later add hot pink dots at the bottom of the border when we found out the baby was a girl. I was so sure she came from heaven that I painted clouds on the ceiling to make her feel instantly at home. I had the best time doing her room. It was one of the ways she and I bonded before her birth.

When I had my second child, I kept the same nursery, but I painted blue over the pink dots since this one was a boy. I was sure the clouds would be pleasurable for him, too. It worked! One simple change was all it took to refresh the existing nursery.

When my third baby came along, everyone in the house had been moved around and it was time for a new nursery. Still enam-

A canopy in pink and taupe from Canopy Panoply (page 44).

Striped fabric was the source of inspiration for the colorful wall stripes of varying thicknesses. For paint details, see the Sticks and Stripes project (page 105).

ored with the idea of a design on the ceiling, since babies spend so much time looking up at it, I created my first canopy ceiling. Canopies are a design I love to this day, and you will see several adaptations of the style in this book. A canopy can be made to work for various ages just by changing the colors.

Part of the fun (and challenge) of painting rooms for older children is involving them in the process. It is nice to know a child's favorite colors, temperament, style, and so on. I try to find a happy balance between parents and children. Parents might appreciate that there's a place to hang artwork or pictures from school. Kids love a border that makes them smile. I try to use patterns low on the walls when painting children's room, since they appreciate a kid's-eye view. Chalkboards and bulletin boards add utility to a room and are great for collecting photographs and messages from friends and relations. Personalizing the room in these ways does much to give a child a sense of belonging.

"Let your **child decide the direction**, not your interior decorator. "

part 1

about
paint

Cool colors were used in the Mermaid's Bower room. For paint details, see the Mermaid's Bower project (page 101).

The fabric source for the scroll border in the Mermaid's room.

WHAT PAINT CAN DO

If you've never painted a room before, there's no better time to start than in a child's nursery or bedroom. Your child is constantly changing, so celebrate this evolution. Mark the first time he sleeps through the night, or the first time she has a sleepover. Celebrate her messy, wonderful march into who she is.

Paint may seem like a permanent step, but the truth is that you can always repaint. This book will show you how to add simple changes to help your children's rooms grow with them. Painting is simple and can be done and redone in multiple layers, so you can avoid having to scrape down

Warm colors in a bathroom.
For paint details, see the
Royal Treatment project
(page 67).

bunny wallpaper or disassemble the canopy bed when your
child outgrows them.

The range of colors can be overwhelming. (The
Benjamin Moore company alone makes more than 3,000
paint colors.) But don't worry—it's just paint after all, and
your child probably has some ideas that will help you to
narrow down the choices. Children are fearless: think about
the instinct that makes them scribble a line of crayon over
a living room wall. Everything is a possible surface, so let
their creativity loose.

Closeup of star from the same bathroom.

You can find motifs everywhere. In this case, the quilted alligator inspired a stencil.

The finished stencil of the alligator. For paint details, see the Creature Feature project (page 65).

If you flip through a decorating magazine, you might see a child's room with an antique brass bed, shelves of orderly toys, or everything down to the doorknobs in a subdued shade of pink. This is not what we're aiming for—let your child decide the direction, not your interior decorator. It's okay if the room isn't perfect, and if everything doesn't fit neatly into a circus or princess theme. Chances are that your daughter likes tea parties and soccer, and your son elephants and sailboats. There's no need to box them into one theme. These are rooms to live in, muck up, reorganize, and set in order again. Here are some of the things that painting your child's room can do:

Change her mood. Unfortunately, not all temper tantrums can be waved away with a can of blue paint. Still, research has shown that colors do affect our moods. Cool colors (grays, greens, and blues) are said to be calming, while warm colors (reds, oranges, and yellows) are energizing and invigorating. A cool color seems to recede (the blue-gray of the ocean) while a warm color advances (a bright red barn). One study showed that looking at the color blue reduced blood pressure and heart rate, while people reacted to red with an increase in adrenaline. Even if everything in your wardrobe is khaki, your child's room is a fun place to try out sunflower yellow or lime green.

Give him a safe haven. Children's rooms should be a place to hide when the world outside is just a little too big. By personalizing his room, you'll give him a cozy space. Everyone needs a shelter, and you can make his a soothing and safe hideaway. Make it a gentle place where dreams aren't far away. If he loves his own bed, he'll be less likely to clamber into yours!

Mark her growth. Think about all the ways you note your child's growth: do you have a clay imprint of her foot when she was a newborn, or a baby book detailing her first steps and first word? Your child's wall can be a living surface for celebrating her growth. Paint on a height chart and mark her development against the wall, writing in the date. Make a border of progressive handprints, or use footprints and add one every time her shoe size goes up.

Decorative cattail growth chart. For paint details, see the Creature Feature project (page 65).

Green vertical stripes and a dotted pink canopy. For paint details, see the Peppy Preppy project (page 55).

A painted headboard is inexpensive and easy to do. For paint details, see the Painted Headboard project (page 111).

It's also easy to paint a garden wall. For paint details, see the Garden Girl project (page 119).

Provide a quick fix or a slow change. Sometimes you want a quick shot of change. If that's what you're after, you can paint a simple stripe or border, or add stencils. At other times, it's nice to spend hours getting lost in the physical act of working with your hands. If you crave the comfort of getting your hands messy, you can tackle the bigger projects in this book, like painting wide swathes of color or detailing freehand images.

Add a cheap fix. Paint is quite inexpensive compared with other dramatic decorative measures. It's frustrating to spend a lot of money on something your child will probably break or scuff up. Paint is durable and costs very little, so don't buy a headboard—paint one!

Bond with your children. Painting is a great way to do something active with your child. When he's younger, you can give him simple tasks like laying down the drop cloth and coating the roller. When you're working on a twelve-year-old's room, hand her a paintbrush. She can take pride in the fact that she sponged the clouds on the ceiling or filled in the sailboat stencil.

Offer up adventure. Children are endlessly curious and sometimes get frustrated when they can't explore everything at once. So make her room a place of discovery. Add circus stripes, sailor's knots, or jungle leaves. Paint a canopy for a bed that feels as if it's from another world.

Soothe yourself. Chances are, you're going to spend hours in the nursery or your toddler's room. Make it a place that is comfortable to be in—even at 3:00 in the morning. Newborns aren't affected by color, so a simple, soft nursery is calming for a harried parent.

Be happily imperfect. The best part about painting is the ability to create inconsistency and variation of colors. When you are painting a border or an entire wall, it is nice for it to look not too perfect. It will make it your own. When I think I have made a mistake, I keep painting. Later, when I look for what I thought was a mistake, I cannot find it. Do not be too hard on yourself, and remember to have fun creating. It is the process of creating this child's room you will remember, not the mistakes! This will also help your children feel that in their art there is no need to be perfect too!

Cool colors were used in this freehand border. For paint details, see the Catch a Wave project (page 107).

A cow's head on the wall offers a touch of the unexpected. For paint details, see the Rugby Stripe project (page 89).

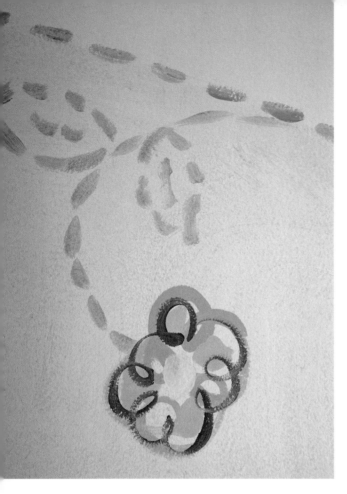

The inspiration for the painted flower design was taken from a quilt. For paint details, see the Be Mine, Flower Vine project (page 81).

The quilt that inspired the painted flowers.

THE CREATIVE PROCESS

There are endless places to find inspiration for decorating your child's room, and dreaming up the design is half the fun. Think about what you and your child love. Inspiration can come from a cherished family heirloom, a worn stuffed animal, even the details and shape of the room itself. Does your child collect shells or stamps? What shirt has holes, what storybook is the most dog-eared, what color crayon is worn down to the nub? There are no rules here, so just let loose and have fun with it—write on the wall or paint freehand. Here are some unexpected sources of design inspiration:

Her favorite vacation. Does she love camping? Paint a nighttime sky on the ceiling, with the names of constellations. Does she hate leaving the beach? Paint waves, palm trees, even a tan sand floor. For the room of a boy who's crazy about surfing, I painted waves on the walls all across the room.

A special blanket. Blankies are important. After all, what would Linus be without his tattered blanket? In a boy's room, I used the blue and white squares of a beloved quilt as inspiration, painting blue and white checkered squares on the walls. For a girl's room, I looked at the beautiful, saturated colors in an Indian-style quilt. The room's pale pink stripes and green-painted headboard echo the colors in the quilt.

A book. What's her most-requested bedtime story? If it's *Madeline*, you could easily replicate the book's key details and primary-color palette. Stencil ivy on the wall and paint the

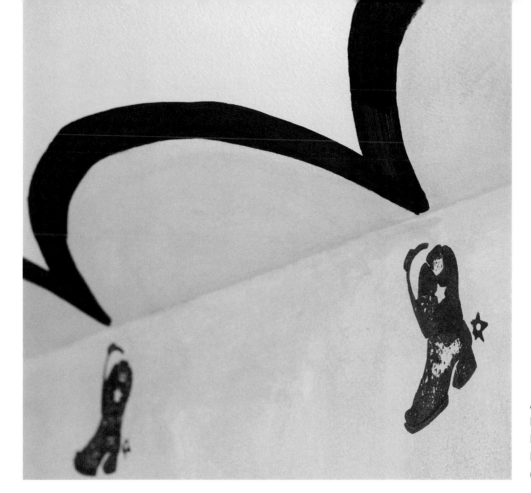

A stencil inspired by a boy's favorite boots. For paint details, see the Buckin' Bronco project (page 87).

walls yellow to mimic the famous orphanage. If it's *The Story of Babar*, add a border of elephants marching across the walls.

The room itself. Look to the architectural details of your home. In an attic nursery, I painted vertical stripes on the walls and pink on the ceiling to accentuate the eaves. If you don't have interesting architectural details, you can add them to keep the room from being a plain white box. In a boy's room, brown horizontal stripes on the wall can add interest and be reminiscent of a log cabin.

A worn pair of cowboy boots. For a young boy's room, we found inspiration in his favorite pair of shoes—black and red leather cowboy boots. A red lasso loops around the ceiling, and boot stencils dance across the tops of the walls.

The favorite cowboy boots.

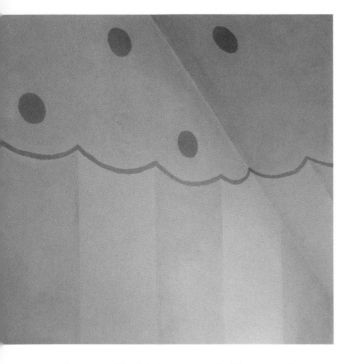

A canopy with pink dots goes well with green stripes. For paint details, see the Peppy Preppy project (page 55).

The tools you will need for stenciling an initial on the wall. For paint details, see the Monogram Me project (page 37).

An old fishing buoy. Any object can provide inspiration. I found an old, weathered buoy and it inspired an entire room. I used a lake-blue wash of color on the walls and painted a fishing lure with a fishing line running across the wall.

Her favorite season. Does she hate winter? Bring spring-time early with flowers on the wall and a sunny blue sky with puffy white clouds. Does she look forward to fall? Paint an oak tree with red and orange leaves.

Your childhood room. Think about your old bedroom. What was your favorite part? Were the walls a color that still reminds you of home, or did you doodle flowers on your doorjamb? Pass it on.

Her imagination. Children are drawn to imaginary beings. If she loves mermaids, paint squiggles on the top of the wall to give an underwater effect.

His name. Make the room really personalized! Monogram a wall with his initials, or paint a sign saying "Chris's Place." Since you liked the name enough to give it to your child, putting it on the wall is not too big a commitment.

Her collections and curiosities. If she has a stamp collection, stencil stamps around the room. If she loves birds, give her a flock on the walls. This could be simple black silhouettes of seagulls or detailed pictures of blue herons. If he collects toy cars, you can stencil cars racing along the bottom of the walls.

Watery blue curlicues suggest the sea. For paint details, see the Mermaid's Bower project (page 101).

PAINT BASICS

Here is a tutorial on all you need to know before you tackle a painting project.

Safety Tips

There are a few necessary steps to ensure that your project is child-friendly:

1 Make sure the workspace is well ventilated.

2 When sanding, wear a mask to prevent breathing in particles and dust.

3 When working with oil- or alcohol-based paint or paint stripper, wear a safety mask to protect you from fumes.

4 Watch out for lead: if your home is older (built before 1960), its walls may have been painted with lead paint.

Painted waves bring in another world. For paint details, see the Catch a Wave project (page 107).

Apricot wash stripe with green detail. For paint details, see the Rugby Stripe project (page 91).

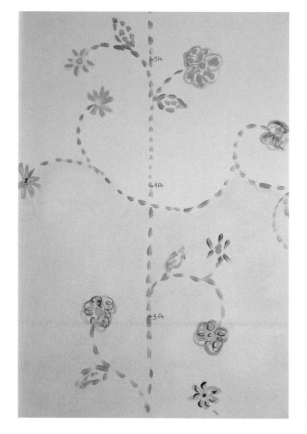

Vine-patterned growth chart painted freehand to mimic quilting stitches. For paint details, see the Be Mine, Flower Vine project (page 81).

Lead paint is very dangerous to both pregnant women and children, so you'll want to get rid of it or contain it. Get any interior or exterior walls that you are planning to redo tested for lead. Follow the guidelines in your area for lead containment or removal. This is a job for a professional, so check with a local paint supplier or your local health department to find a professional trained in removing lead. If your paint has lead in it, don't scrape or sand it, as this can scatter dangerous particles.

5 Use a low-odor paint. There are many great environmentally friendly paints out there! Use them.

Paint Types

All paints consist of pigment (the powder that contains the color), binder (which carries the pigment), and diluent (which dilutes paint so that it is manageable). Paints are either oil-based or water-based. Water-based paints are nontoxic and easy to clean up, so we recommend using them for children's rooms. Sunny's Goodtime Paints are latex, which is water-based. The following are some pros and cons of each type of paint:

◆ **Oil-based paint:** Oil-based paints are the traditional material for decorative painting, mainly because they dry more slowly and so give you more time to fix mistakes. They have a very durable finish that can handle wear and tear. The cons for this type of paint are that the slower drying time means a longer wait between coats and cleanup is trickier: you'll need paint thinner. Also, there are more safety issues, since oil-based paints give off fumes and are flammable.

- **Water-based paint:** Water-based paints include latex, enamel, and acrylic paints. The main benefit of working with water-based paints is that they don't give off fumes. Other pros: these paints have a faster drying time, are easier to clean up (just use water), and are safer for the environment since they don't contain solvents and can be thinned with water instead of chemicals. The cons: the faster drying time leaves less room for mistakes when you're working on a new technique or a large surface.

Paint Coats

- **Primer:** The first coat used on an unpainted (or stripped and sanded) surface.

- **Basecoat:** Any layer of paint before the finish.

- **Finish:** The color-saturated paint; the main course. Some tones, like bright reds and pinks, often need more than one coat of finish.

Types of Finishes

- **Flat:** A finish with no gloss.

- **Matte:** A finish with little gloss.

- **Eggshell:** A finish with a slight sheen.

- **Semi-gloss/high-gloss:** Quite shiny/very shiny finishes.

The topcoat is the last layer of paint to be applied. The topcoat can be the finish or a decorative coat over the finish (like a varnish). Some types of topcoats are as follows:

A 12" (30.5 cm) pink stripe with green trim. For paint details, see the Cotton Candy Stripes project (page 96).

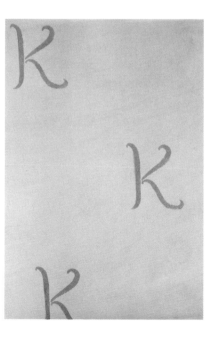

A monogram personalizes a room. For details, see the Monogram Me project (page 40).

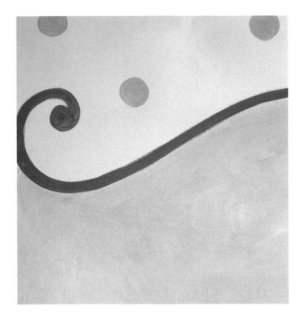

A painted curlicue. For paint details, see the Canopy Panoply project (page 48).

Varnish: A clear topcoat that determines the level of gloss on the wall.

Glaze: A transparent, sometimes tinted coat that is applied with a brush over the finish to soften or enhance it.

Wash (colorwash): A thin, high-pigment coat that goes over the finish to enhance it, creating a wash effect. It's similar to a glaze, but it is more opaque so it covers more of the base color. It is applied with a rag and dries quickly. By layering colorwashes on top of each other, you can create more depth.

Clearcoat: A colorless coat similar to a varnish that changes the level of gloss.

MATERIALS

Here are the tools that you should round up before you start painting. They will ensure that the whole process, from prepping the room to cleaning up, goes smoothly.

Brushes. You can use nylon or polyester brushes for latex paints, while oil-based paints should be applied with a natural-bristle brush. I like to use a 2½" (6.5 cm) natural-bristle brush for all my projects, however, whether I am using latex or oil. To clean it after using latex-based paint, immediately wash the brush with soap and water.

Drop cloths. Use a canvas drop cloth, an old sheet, or disposable plastic drop cloths to protect the floor and

Natural bristle brushes.

furniture from paint drops. I prefer canvas, since plastic tarps often get tangled.

• **Grout.** A thin, coarse, mortar. Use nonsanded tile grout for mixing chalkboard paint.

• **Paint rollers.** Paint rollers are very handy for getting at hard-to-reach places and covering a large surface evenly and quickly. The painting surface of the roller is called a sleeve or cover. The length of the sleeve varies; pick a larger one for a larger wall surface. You'll also want an extension pole for the roller.

• **Roller pan.** A roller pan is a shallow metal pan with a ramp. You run the roller up and down the ramp to coat the sleeve with paint evenly.

Drop cloth.

Roller pan with paint roller.

Blue painter's tape.

• **Primer.** Primer fills and seals an unfinished surface. It will help paint adhere to the surface.

♦ **Tape.** Use tape to block out the surfaces you want to paint in order to shield windows or floors from the paint you're applying. Tape is also useful for holding stencils in place. I like Scotch® Blue Decorative Painter's Tape made by 3M, as it's less likely to pull off existing paint than a tackier tape. I use 2" (5 cm) brown paper tape for painting stripes.

♦ **Rags.** You'll definitely want a pile of rags handy for wiping up drips and spills and cleaning your brushes.

Paper tape.

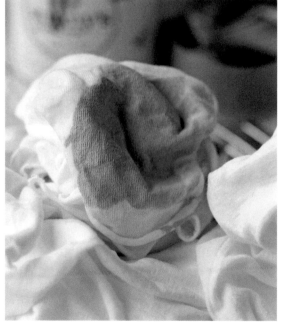

White cotton rags.

White cotton rags or old T-shirts are best. Dyed rags can rub off on the walls.

◆ **Ladder.** A definite necessity if you're working from floor to ceiling. I recommend a lightweight ladder; fiberglass is a bit sturdier than aluminum. A 4' (1.20 m) ladder lets you reach most ceiling heights with a roller and an extension pole.

◆ **Level.** A bubble level allows you to make a straight vertical or horizontal line.

◆ **Mixing cup.** Keep a cup handy for mixing or diluting paints.

Use a ladder with a tray to keep supplies at hand.

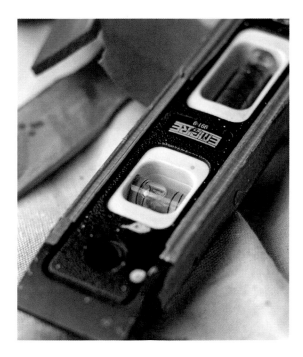

A level is a big help when drawing straight lines.

Mixing cups are good for mixing glazes.

Chalks are very useful for sketching out areas to paint and designs.

An artist's brush is used to paint freehand details.

A tape measure comes in handy for planning designs.

◆ **Chalk.** Use colored chalk to mark off patterns such as stripes or freehand drawings.

◆ **Artist's brush.** I like to use a #10 or #12 artist's brush for freehand painting. These are thinner than paintbrushes for walls, and allow you to paint details easily.

◆ **Measuring tape.** Use a measuring tape to measure and mark off stripes, plaids, or panels.

◆ **Sponge.** I like to use a sea sponge for stenciling as well as for applying glazes.

A sea sponge gives paint a unique texture.

Checkerboard is one of many choices
to liven up a room. From Little Boy Blue
(page 77).

HOW TO USE THIS BOOK

There are many projects in this book to choose from.
You might want to start off with something simple,
like a soft colorwash for a new nursery or a stencil for a
six-year-old's room. If you just want to get your feet wet,
try painting a single wall. Or paint the ceiling a lighter
shade of the wall color; it will make the ceiling look
higher. One of the more imaginative projects that's fairly
simple to do is a painted headboard (page 111). Or, if
you are itching to take on a more challenging project,
you could paint a checkerboard wall (page 77) or a
freehand lasso border (page 131).

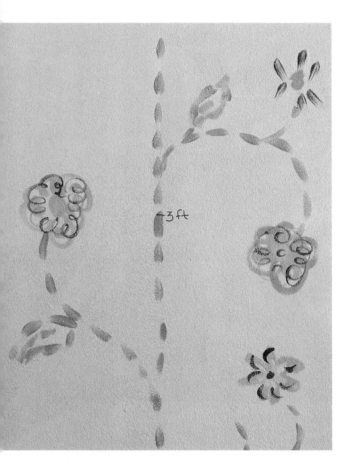

A flower vine might be just what your youngster would like. From Be Mine, Flower Vine (page 81).

If you're not sure what you'd like to paint yet, flip through the book for ideas and inspiration. You can use it loosely: take what you like from a project and leave the rest. Maybe you like the idea of loops with dots underneath, but you'd rather they were loops with flowers beneath. Go for it! This book is all about creating unusual rooms that feel like home to you and your child.

The chapters are organized by age: nurseries for wee ones; rooms to play and grow in for children ages 4 through 8; and rooms to think and dream in for children ages 9 through 12. Of course, you can pick and choose projects from the different sections and you can adapt the colors and ideas from these projects to suit your own home, furnishings, and fabrics. Mix-and-match color options are included with many of the projects.

I hope that you'll use this book again and again. I've painted and repainted my own daughter's room five times—and she's only nine! As your child grows, you can look here for ways to help the room evolve—a nursery border can be striped over when a child outgrows elephants or bunnies, for example. These rooms will never have to be completely overhauled. But once you see how simple it is to change a room with colorwash or a freehand border, you may be tempted to try a new pattern, a new border, or a new color before your newborn is out of diapers or before your five-year-old outgrows her growth chart. Simple but striking changes will keep the rooms fresh and your children cheery.

PREPARING THE ROOM FOR PAINTING

Painting a room is pretty easy, but you need to prep it carefully for success. Check out the walls you are going to paint. The ideal surface for paint is hard, smooth, dry, and clean. If your walls are all of these things, the paint will go on easily and last a long time. If the walls have been painted recently and are in good condition, you are ready to start. If the paint is peeling or scuffed, you should do some prep work before you begin painting. Otherwise, stains and marks that are already on the wall will show through your new work.

1 Vacuum or dust all surfaces (especially the tops of doors and windows).

2 Walls collect a lot of grime and dust and should be washed down thoroughly. Scrub surfaces and wall marks with water or a cleaning product. (I prefer the Mr. Clean Magic Eraser®, which works, well, like magic on wall surfaces.) Let the surface dry thoroughly.

3 Scrape off any peeling paint. If it's only a small area, you can scrape it off and sand it down until it is smooth. If it seems lower than the rest of the surface, mix a bit of spackle and water until it is the consistency of paint, and paint it over the rough surface. Sand it down when dry. A large flaking paint surface will require a paint stripper.

4 If the plaster in the wall is noticeably uneven, fill in the cracks with spackle. Fill the cracks so that they are raised slightly above the surface of the rest of the wall. Let the spackle dry and then sand it lightly until the surface is even.

5 Prime all areas that have been spackled and sanded. (You don't need to apply primer to clean walls that have already been painted, only to new, unpainted areas.) A shellac- or alcohol-based primer will help the paint to adhere to the surface. Now you're ready to start painting!

Painted lure on a boy's wall

"You can give your children a room of color and lightness, **a bright, safe space** where they are free to grow and explore."

newborn through age 3

nurseries
for wee ones

marching elephants

TECHNIQUES

colorwash, stencil, freehand

COLORWASHED WALLS AND A JOVIAL BORDER of elephants turn a small, simple room into a happy nursery. The elephant's multi-colored blanket ties in with the other colors in the room, and the border pattern is complete with a stenciled crown and baby-blue dots. The inspiration for this room was actually a lovely piece of wrapping paper.

featured colors

- **Light blue-gray latex eggshell basecoat**
- **Sunny's Goodtime Little Boy Blue Colour Wash**
- **Various acrylic tube paints for the elephant stencils and freehand trim**
- **Light blue latex eggshell for the dot stencils**

opposite: A parade of elephants and crowns decorates the walls at a height that the baby can see from the crib.

right: The elephant was stenciled and then detailed by hand for additional color.

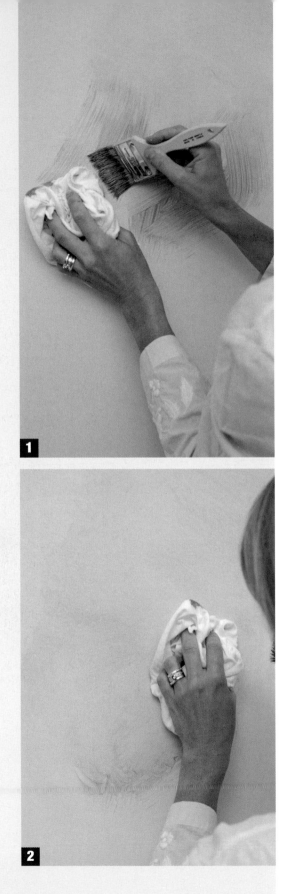

GENERAL INSTRUCTIONS

1 Paint the walls in the base color. Let them dry for at least 5 days.

2 Colorwash the walls in Sunny's Goodtime Little Boy Blue Colour Wash (see colorwash instructions below).

3 Stencil the elephants in a band around the room at about crib height in pencil or chalk, leaving room for crowns or whatever decorations you want in between the elephants. Stencil the crowns.

4 Add color to the elephants by painting them freehand to make them more interesting.

INSTRUCTIONS FOR COLORWASH

1 Apply the colorwash to a clean wall with a 2" (5 cm) natural bristle brush (Photo 1).

2 As though you're washing a window, use a clean white cotton rag to blend the wash, "washing" evenly to prevent dark lines of colorwash from forming at the edges of your ragging (Photo 2).

3 "Wash" the paint on in a random fashion. Avoid consistent up and down or side to side application, which could result in a noticeable pattern.

tip

Take excess paint off the brush with the rag, and stipple carefully into the corners with the brush.

Photo 1. Apply the colorwash with a 2" (5 cm) brush.

Photo 2. Use the cotton rag to spread and blend the color.

Mix and match

A pink wall with gray elephants is adorable.

- White latex eggshell basecoat
- Sunny's Goodtime Bubblegum Pink Colour Wash combination color*
- Sunny's French Gray Colour Wash for the elephants
- Acrylic craft paints in various colors: lavender, green, tangerine, and medium blue

  *Note: To create Sunny's Goodtime Bubblegum Pink Colour Wash, mix 16 oz. Palm Beach Pink Colour Wash with 8 oz. Sunny's Goodtime Ruby Red Glaze.

More mix and match

Or try pale green walls with gray elephants with the following.

- White latex eggshell basecoat
- Sunny's Goodtime Lizard Lime Colour Wash for the wall
- Sunny's French Gray Colour Wash for the elephants
- Acrylic craft paint in various colors: green, tangerine, lavender

GROWING INTO THE ROOM

This border can be adapted easily as the child grows. For example, imagine painting over the elephants with a large band of color and washing below the band with a deeper blue. You might also add a chalkboard wall.

A pink and French Gray variation on the elephant theme.

A pale green wall with a French gray elephant.

dot, dot, dot

TECHNIQUES

colorwash, stencil

featured colors for the bedroom

- **Off white latex eggshell basecoat**
- **Sunny's Goodtime Avocado Colour Wash combination color for the wall finish***
- **Sunny's Goodtime Palm Beach Pink Colour Wash for the dots**

  *Note: To create Sunny's Goodtime Avocado Colour Wash, mix 12 oz. Sunny's Goodtime Lizard Lime Colour Wash with 12 oz. Sunny's Goodtime Gator Green Glaze.

DOT STENCILS ARE ONE OF THE most popular items sold at Sunny's Goodtime Paints, not only because the stencil is an easy decorative painting project to try, but also because the simple dot pattern works in rooms for boys and girls of any age. The walls in baby Katie's nursery are finished with an avocado colorwash. The pink dots—inspired by the dots on the green and pink window shade—add perfect punctuation to the room.

The walls in the bathroom adjoining Katie's room were an uninspired off-white. They livened up considerably with the addition of the initial S—for Katie Smith—stenciled on in pink.

above: Closeup of avocado colorwashed walls with pink dots.

opposite: Colorwashed walls with dot stencil carry over the design from the shade.

right: Dots on the window shade provided the theme.

An uninspired bathroom was enlivened with a Bubblegum Pink S stencil.

INSTRUCTIONS FOR DOT STENCIL

1 Paint the room with the basecoat; let dry for at least 5 days.

2 Lightly dip your sponge into the glaze and then tap directly on top of the stencil.

3 Space about 12" to 18" (30.5 to 46 cm) apart, or from finger to elbow.

4 Remove the stencil and repeat until you have finished the entire room.

featured colors for bathroom

- Off-white latex eggshell basecoat
- Sunny's Goodtime Bubblegum Pink Colour Wash combination color for the S stencil*

*Note: To create Sunny's Goodtime Bubblegum Pink, mix 16 oz. Palm Beach Pink Colour Wash with 8 oz. Sunny's Goodtime Ruby Red Glaze.

monogram me!

TECHNIQUES

colorwash, stencil

featured colors

- **Off white (with a yellow tint) latex eggshell basecoat**
- **Sunny's Goodtime Palm Beach Pink Colour Wash**
- **Sunny's Goodtime Bubblegum Pink Colour Wash combination color for the letter stencil***

*Note: To create Sunny's Goodtime Bubblegum Pink, mix 16 oz. Palm Beach Pink Colour Wash with 8 oz. Sunny's Goodtime Ruby Red Glaze.

IT'S NEVER TOO EARLY TO ENCOURAGE self-awareness in your baby. Paint a monogram of her initials on the wall in a lovely script or print and she'll never forget who she is. The walls of baby Hattie's nursery are washed in a soft pink, and her first initial, H, is lovingly stenciled around the room in a slightly darker shade. I created this stencil to match the lettering on a beautiful quilt given to Hattie by her grandmother. The stencils appear to be randomly placed around the walls. I used chalk to mark the placement before painting the stencils on.

A quilt inspired the H monogram.

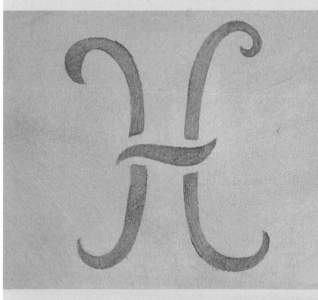

The completed monogram, a darker pink on a soft pink colorwashed wall.

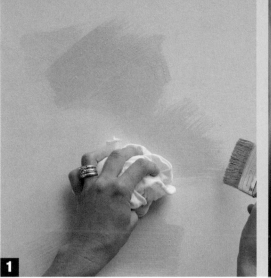

INSTRUCTIONS
FOR LETTER STENCILS

1 Paint the room with the off-white basecoat. Let dry for at least 5 days.

2 Apply pink colorwash to the wall using a 2" (5 cm) brush; use a clean cotton rag to blend in the paint for the desired colorwash effect (Photo 1).

3 When the wash is completely dry, apply the stencil paint. Hold the stencil template in place and dab a bit of paint on the side of the stencil to remove any excess from the brush. This helps keep the paint from bleeding under the stencil.

4 Stipple or lightly tap the pink wash inside the stencil area, being careful to apply an even layer of product (Photo 2).

5 Carefully remove the stencil and—voila!—the letter H (Photos 3 and 4).

Photo 1. Apply the pink colorwash to the wall, using a cotton rag.

Photo 2. Stipple the pink wash inside the stencil.

Photo 3. Prepare to remove the stencil.

Photo 4. Remove the stencil.

opposite: The monogrammed wall behind the baby's crib.

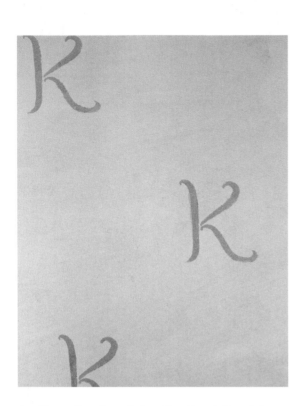

Monogram materials.

A gold stencil on Sunny's Goodtime French Gray Colour Wash.

Mix and match

Other color combinations might include:

- Gold stencil on Sunny's Goodtime French Gray Colour Wash

- Sunny's Goodtime Pumpkin Colour Wash stencil on Pumpkin Colour Wash

- Sunny's Goodtime Ocean Age Aging Glaze stencil on Ocean Age Aging Glaze

Sunny's Goodtime Pumpkin Colour Wash stenciled on Pumpkin Colour Wash.

Sunny's Goodtime Ocean Age Aging Glaze Stenciled on Ocean Age Aging Glaze.

lavender's blue

TECHNIQUES:

striated colorwash

featured colors

- **Pale lavender latex eggshell basecoat**
- **Sunny's Goodtime Lavender Colour Wash combination color (diluted with water, 6 oz. water to 24 oz. paint mixture)***

*Note: To create Sunny's Goodtime Lavender Colour Wash, mix 12 oz. Sunny's Goodtime La-La Lilac Colour Wash with 12 oz. Sunny's Goodtime Plainly Plum Glaze.

LAVENDER'S BLUE, DILLY DILLY, lavender's green. At least that's what the folk song suggests. But in this baby girl's nursery, lavender's lavender! With yellow bedding, draperies, and furniture already in the room, lavender, a complementary color to yellow on the color wheel, seemed an inspired choice for the walls. Replace the bed and the bunny bedding, and this room will take her from toddler to tween to teen. The lavender colorwash was applied here with a 2" (5 cm) natural bristle brush for a striated effect.

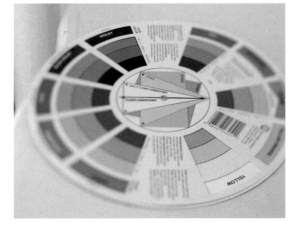

above: On the color wheel, complementary colors are directly opposite each other, for example, purple and yellow.

right: A colorwash applied with a natural fairly dry bristle brush creates a striated effect.

INSTRUCTIONS FOR STRIATED COLORWASH

1 Paint the room with the basecoat. Let dry for at least 5 days.

2 To create the striated colorwash, use a wide natural bristle brush, applying the Lavender Colour Wash with a fairly dry brush.

Mix and match

For a brushed-on green glaze:

- Medium lime green latex eggshell basecoat

- Sunny's Goodtime Avocado Colour Wash combination color brushed on top*

  *Note: To create Sunny's Goodtime Avocado Colour Wash, mix 12 oz. Sunny's Goodtime Lizard Lime Colour Wash with 12 oz. Sunny's Goodtime Gator Green Glaze.

More mix and match

For a brushed-on blue glaze:

- Medium purple-blue latex eggshell basecoat

- Sunny's Goodtime Marine Glaze brushed on top

right: Sunny's Goodtime Marine Glaze is another choice; shown over a purple-blue basecoat.

opposite: Lavender colorwash on the walls.

Sunny's Goodtime Avocado Colour Wash is an alternate wash color over a light green basecoat.

canopy panoply

A CANOPY BORDER WORKS ESPECIALLY WELL in this nursery, and it's hard to outgrow the sophisticated color palette of pink and taupe! Freehand initials personalize the room even more. I love the pink and brown color combination in the cotton blanket, which also inspired a vertical pinstripe pattern that might be used in a larger nursery (see page 49).

TECHNIQUES

freehand canopy, dot stencil, colorwash

featured colors

- **Off white latex eggshell basecoat**
- **Sunny's Goodtime Palm Beach Pink Colour Wash combination color below the border***
- **Sunny's Goodtime Toffee Glaze combination color for the border and dots***

*Note: To create Sunny's Goodtime Bubblegum Pink Colour Wash, mix 16 oz. Palm Beach Pink Colour Wash with 8 oz. Sunny's Goodtime Ruby Red Glaze. To create Sunny's Goodtime Toffee Glaze, mix 10 oz. Original Antique Aging Glaze with 14 oz. Sunny's Goodtime Cappuccino Glaze.

right: A monogram adds detail.

opposite: A pale pink and taupe color palette is easy on the eye and updates easily for a growing girl.

Dots in the canopy echo buttons in the window treatment.

INSTRUCTIONS FOR CANOPY

1 Paint the walls with the basecoat of taupe and let dry for at least 5 days.

2 Sketch the canopy pattern on the wall with colored chalk. I like to make the canopy extend about 16" to 20" (40.6 cm to 50.8 cm) from the ceiling, depending on the height of the ceiling. The higher the ceiling, the farther I come down with the canopy. This canopy border is only 16" (40.6 cm) from the ceiling because the ceiling is rather low. I sketch on the wall with chalk rather than on paper because it's important to draw to the scale of the room. Using chalk makes it easy to change the pattern as you go; no need to fret about mistakes, just wipe them off and do it over until you have the design to your liking.

3 Apply pink colorwash with a 2" (5 cm) brush beneath the canopy outline (Photo 1).

4 Use a clean cotton rag to blend in the colorwash, being careful as you work within the small area of the swirls (Photo 2).

5 Let the colorwash dry about 24 hours.

6 Use a #16 artist's brush to paint the toffee scroll over the chalk markings.

7 Hold the paint-product lid in your free hand as you work for easy access (Photo 3).

Photo 1. Apply the pink colorwash.

Photo 2. Blend the colorwash with a rag.

Photo 3. Paint the scroll, using the paint-product lid in your free hand as a palette.

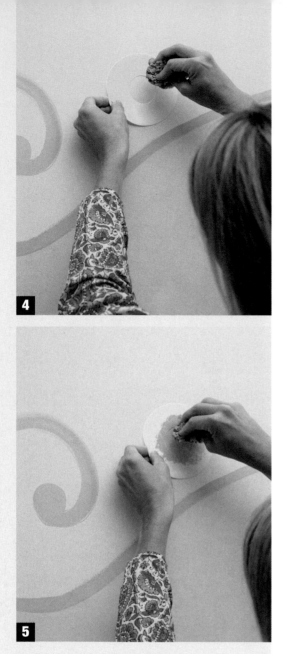

8 Hold a dot stencil against the wall and fill in with paint using a sea sponge. Fill in the dots with toffee glaze, dabbing paint generously onto the stencil. Space the dots about 12" (30.5 cm) apart (Photos 4 and 5).

Mix and match

The same canopy works just as well in a boy's nursery.

- White latex eggshell basecoat for the wall
- Sunny's Goodtime Little Boy Blue Colour Wash is washed on the ceiling
- Sunny's Goodtime Marine Glaze washed below the border
- Light beige latex eggshell for the dots
- Medium beige latex eggshell for the border

Photo 4. Hold the stencil against the wall.

Photo 5. Dab on the paint with a sea sponge.

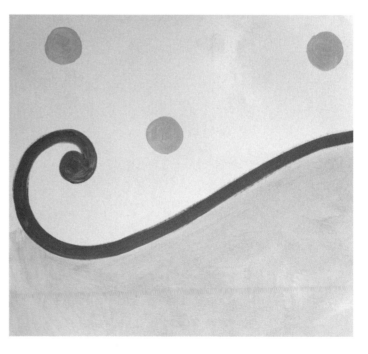

Closeup of the painted canopy in more muted colors for the boy's room.

vertical pinstripe nursery

HERE'S ANOTHER USE OF THE PINK and brown color combination in the cotton blanket, a vertical pinstripe pattern that might be used in a larger nursery. The traditional stripe with a little detail works wonders. It's more effort but well worth it. Details always are! The chocolate brown pinstripe grounds the Toffee Glaze stripe, and the pink pinstripe adds lively contrast.

The same lively fabric design inspires pink stripes rather than a canopy.

right: Closeup shows wide Toffee Glaze stripe with pink and chocolate brown pinstripes.

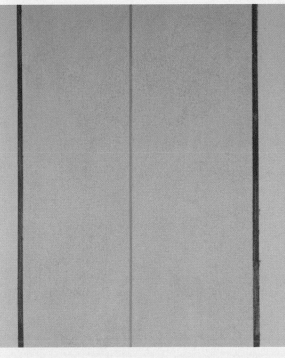

To start, paint the room with the off white basecoat. Let dry for 5 days.

INSTRUCTIONS FOR VERTICAL PINSTRIPES

1 Measure 12" (30.5 cm) in from the corner and mark a vertical mark with chalk. Continue measuring and marking around the room at 12" intervals (Photo 1).

2 Align the right side of a strip of 2" (5 cm) brown paper tape along the outside of the chalk line and tape off the line (Photo 2).

3 Tape off the other chalk line for the 12" stripe (Photo 3).

Photo 1. Measure 12" (30.5 cm) from the corner and mark with chalk. Continue marking around the room.

Photo 2. Align tape along the outside of the chalk line.

Photo 3. Tape off the next lines for stripes

opposite: The same taupe and pale pink color scheme, used on these pinstriped walls, will be just as appealing when she's 10 as it is in the nursery.

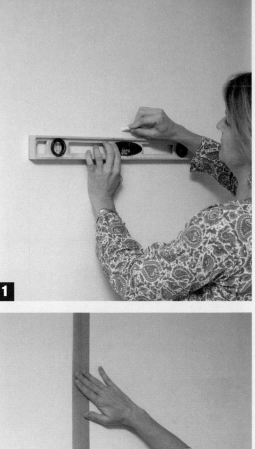

51

4

5

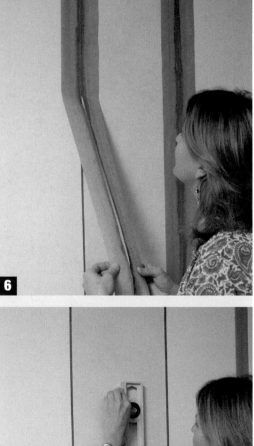

6

7

4 Apply Toffee Glaze with a 2" (5 cm) natural bristle brush onto the wall between the pieces of tape and blend in the paint with a rag to get the desired wash effect (Photo 4).

5 After the Toffee Glaze has dried (this happens quickly, in about 20 minutes), use brown paper tape to tape off the brown pinstripes edging the glazed stripe: align the outside of the pinstripe tape ¼" (6 mm) from the inside of each piece of tape marking the 12" (30.5 cm)-stripe.

6 Use a #12 artist's brush to apply brown paint for the pinstripe (Photo 5).

7 Remove tape to reveal the brown pinstripe (Photo 6).

8 Use a level to find the center of the glazed, 12" (30.5 cm) stripe you just pinstriped in brown and mark the center with chalk (Photo 7). Use the level to draw a vertical line with chalk in center.

Photo 4. Apply the Toffee Glaze to create the 12" (30.5 cm) stripe.

Photo 5. Apply brown paint for the chocolate pinstripe.

Photo 6. Chocolate pinstripes revealed!

Photo 7. Measure and mark the center of the glazed, 12" (30.5 cm) stripe.

tip

A bubble level will let you check that the lines you draw are really vertical.

9 Tape off a stripe ⅛" (3 mm) wide along the chalk line (Photo 8).

10 Use a #8 artist's brush to paint the pink pinstripe (Photo 9).

11 Remove tape to reveal the pink pinstripe (Photo 10). Voila!

12 Continue to mark and paint alternate 12" (30.5 cm) stripes in the room, letting the off-white basecoat show through for the intervening 12" stripes.

Photo 8. Tape off the ⅛"" (3 mm) stripe along the chalk line.

Photo 9. Paint the pink pinstripe.

Photo 10. Voila! Pink stripe revealed.

53

peppy preppy

TECHNIQUES

canopy, stripes, colorwash

featured colors

- **Light green latex eggshell basecoat**
- **Sunny's Goodtime Gator Green Glaze for the 12" (30.5 cm) stripes**
- **Sunny's Goodtime Pumpkin Glaze for the scalloped canopy.**
- **Light rose latex eggshell for the dot stencils**

THIS LIVELY NURSERY EMBRACES one of my favorite color combinations—pink and green! The canopied ceiling completes the room, unifying the disparate elements of angled walls, dormer windows, and a large open space. Green stripes echo the colorful bedding and add just the right finishing touch.

INSTRUCTIONS FOR VERTICAL STRIPES AND CANOPY

1 Paint the room with a light green latex eggshell basecoat. Let dry for at least 5 days.

2 Measure and mark a horizontal line in chalk to be the highest edge of the canopy (points). This might be about 2 feet from the ceiling, depending on the room's height and your preference.

3 Measure another line to be the lowest edge of the canopy (bottom of the scallops) about 2" (5 CM) below the first line.

right: Closeup view of the green colorwashed stripes, with a pink dot canopy above.

opposite: Green stripes and a pink dot canopy add interest above a little girl's crib; the cheerful colors will be suitable as she grows older also.

Marking Off for Vertical Stripes

1 Begin in the corner of the room.

2 Measure 12" (30.5 cm) along the wall from the corner and mark a vertical line for the edge of the stripe with chalk (Photo 1).

3 Continue around the room, measuring 12" (30.5 cm) between chalk marks.

4 If the last stripe in the corner is too wide or too narrow, offset the irregular width by combining the width of the last two stripes and dividing that width in half, using one-half for each stripe. Once the room is complete, you won't notice the off-size width.

5 Use a level to mark the vertical lines with chalk at the 12" (30.5 cm) marks from the start of the canopy (Photo 2).

6 If a painted stripe will butt up to another painted stripe at the corner of the room, or if an unpainted stripe will butt up to another unpainted stripe, halve the width of one stripe so it becomes two stripes at the corner. In effect, you are adding one more stripe.

7 Once you have defined your stripes, mark your canopy scallops in chalk, putting the lowest curve of each scallop in the center of a stripe.

8 Tape off the baseboard trim to protect it, using blue painter's tape.

9 Lay out a drop cloth under the first wall you plan to paint.

10 Tape off the edges of one stripe at a time as you paint, using brown paper tape (Photo 3).

Photo 1. Mark 12" (30 cm) intervals for vertical stripes in chalk.

Photo 2. Mark vertical lines with chalk, using a level.

Photo 3. Tape off edges of stripes with brown paper tape.

Painting the Vertical Stripes

Note: These stripes were painted in another room, but the concept is the same.

1 Brush on the Gator Green glaze in the middle of the stripe (at the top) and then rub it around with a rag, as if you were washing a window. If you begin in the middle of the stripe and work out to the edges of the tape, paint will not bleed under the tape (Photo 4).

2 Colorwash with the same glaze in this manner from the top of the stripe down to the bottom. Use a small brush to colorwash up near the scallops.

3 Remove any excess glaze from the brush with the rag, and then use the brush to stipple the top and bottom edges to achieve a smooth, professional finish. Use a small brush to colorwash up near the scallops.

4 After one stripe has been colorwashed, remove the brown tape and move on to the next stripe (Photo 5).

5 Pull the blue tape off the trim after one whole wall is complete. Pulling tape off is fun, and revealing your neat handiwork gives you a great sense of accomplishment.

6 Finish each wall in the same manner.

Painting the Canopy

1 Glaze the canopy area with Sunny's Goodtime Pumpkin Glaze and let dry.

2 Use an artist's brush and light rose latex eggshell to paint the scalloped border. Use a dot stencil and a brush to paint the dots on the border.

tip

* Use blue tape for protecting the trim, and use brown paper tape for your walls. The brown paper tape is less tacky and will not remove your basecoat.

* Add a stencil to the stripes for a more complex effect.

Photo 4. Brush on the glaze and rub with a rag.

Photo 5. Remove brown tape after painting one stripe.

loop-de-loop

TECHNIQUES

colorwash, freehand, stencil

featured colors

- White latex eggshell basecoat
- Sunny's Goodtime Sunshine Daydream Glaze
- Bright coral latex eggshell for the freehand loop
- Light blue latex eggshell for the dot stencils

AS ANY NEW PARENT KNOWS, HAVING A BABY in the house means keeping a lot of balls in the air. The happy mood of this room was inspired by the soft primary colors on a simple juggling doll. The freehand border is a simple loop-de-loop accented with colorful dot stencils. The walls are colorwashed in yellow and the deep freehand border is red and blue. The dot stencils might also have been painted rosy pink or even some pink and some blue. The loop-de-loop might just as easily have been accented by freehand flowers, echoing the nightstand drawer pull (see next page) or flowers on the picture frame.

opposite: Loop-de-loop room with dot stencil border. The design will work well for an older child's room as well as a nursery.

right: A clown doll inspired the colors and theme of the room.

INSTRUCTIONS FOR LOOP-DE-LOOP ROOM

You can freehand on walls, borders, panels, or furniture. I use a round #10 synthetic artist's brush, because it allows me to control how wide or thin I want a line to be. Practice making freehand loops with your brush and some water on a piece of cardboard first, before you use paint on the wall. To apply freehand loop-de-loop design with paint, follow these easy steps:

1 Paint the room with the basecoat. Let dry for at least 5 days.

2 Glaze the walls with Sunny's Goodtime Sunshine Daydream Glaze. Let dry for one day.

3 Draw your desired loop design with chalk.

4 Use a paper palette to load your brush with coral paint, and paint the design on top of the chalk lines.

5 Chalk marks can be cleaned with a damp rag after the room is completed and the paint has had 24 hours to dry.

6 Add the light blue balls below the loops with a dot stencil.

7 Highlight the stenciled balls with a quick, small brush-stroke of white at the top of each one. This adds dimension.

The loop-de-loop border traipses across a sunny, angled wall.

"A favorite toy, an old pair of cowboy boots, or a special blanket can be the source of your inspiration.**"**

ages 4 through 8

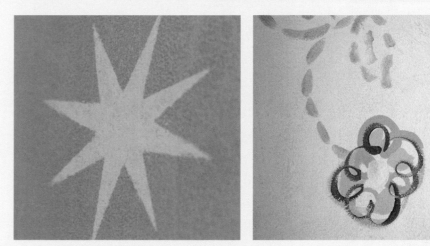

rooms to play and grow in

creature feature

TECHNIQUES

colorwash, stencil

featured colors

- **Medium yellow-green latex eggshell for basecoat**
- **Sunny's Goodtime Gator Green Glaze for the border below the alligators**
- **Custom color combination: mix 4 oz. of medium purple-blue latex eggshell paint with 4 oz. of Sunny's Goodtime Marine Glaze to create the custom color for the alligator stencils**
- **Acrylic tube paints in umber and sienna for cattail growth chart; in red for alligator eyes**

THIS ROOM WAS ALREADY PAINTED a nice spring green and seemed to cry out for . . . well, blue alligators! To tie the other elements of the room together, I made a custom alligator-like stencil, using the creature on a quilt as the pattern. The border at bed-rail height creates an interesting accent that works well with the framed art and decorative bookshelves in the room. The cattail growth chart (page 66) adds a swampy touch. Look, ma, I'm up to here now!

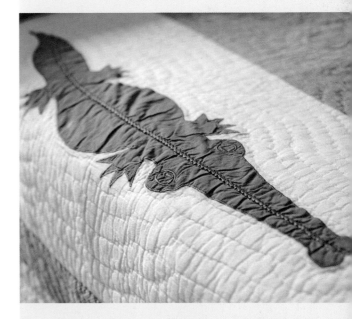

right: The quilted creature inspired the stencil design.

opposite: A blue stencil border at bed-rail height was added on glazed walls that had previously been painted a medium yellow-green.

The cattail growth chart was painted freehand with diluted colors of tube acrylic paints.

GENERAL INSTRUCTIONS

1 Paint the room in the green basecoat or color of your choice; let dry for at least 5 days before glazing.

2 Create the stencil from thin cardboard or thin plastic.

3 Use a bubble ruler and chalk to mark out a border line around the room. Mark stencils equally spaced around the room, on the walls where you want them.

4 Apply the Sunny's Gator Green Glaze to the room from the stenciled areas down, with a brush and rag. Let the glaze dry. This will take about 20 minutes.

5 Mix the custom color for the alligators and apply it to the stenciled designs with a small sponge.

6 When dry, add red eyes to alligators and any other features you want, and red dots between gators.

7 Sketch the cattail growth chart at a convenient height for your child and paint in with muted acrylic tube paints.

the royal treatment

TECHNIQUES

colorwash, freehand

featured colors
for the bedroom

- **Pale yellow latex eggshell basecoat**
- **Sunny's Goodtime Cantaloupe Glaze combination color for the panel***
- **Sunny's Goodtime Bubblegum Pink Glaze combination color for the scroll****

*Note: To create Sunny's Goodtime Cantaloupe Glaze, mix 12 oz. Sunny's Goodtime Pumpkin Glaze with 12 oz. Sunny's Goodtime Sunshine Daydream Glaze.

**To create Sunny's Goodtime Bubblegum Pink, mix 16 oz. Sunny's Goodtime Palm Beach Pink Colour Wash with 8 oz. Sunny's Goodtime Ruby Red Glaze.

WHETHER SHE'S INTO CINDERELLA OR NOT, a charming scroll pattern and colorwashed panel creates an especially inviting room. Raspberry glaze spruces up the dull pink wall in the bathroom, which adjoins the bedroom. Stenciled, bright yellow stars add an enchanting finishing detail.

above: A freehand monogram echoes the lines of the painted furniture in the room and adds a personal touch.

right: Bubblegum Pink swirls on Cantaloupe Glaze; wispy freehand swirls add a feminine detail.

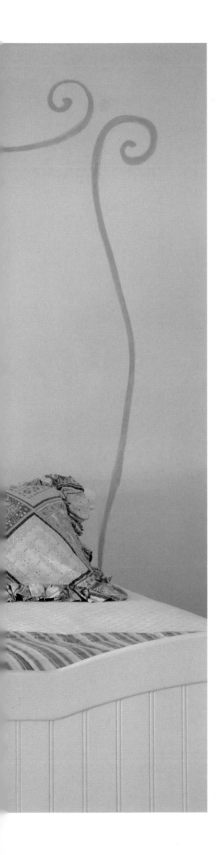

INSTRUCTIONS FOR BEDROOM

1 Paint the room with a pale yellow basecoat; let dry for at least 5 days.

2 The scroll pattern, which connects the twin beds, is drawn on with colored chalk and painted freehand with an artist's brush and the Bubblegum Pink Glaze.

3 Once the scroll pattern is painted and dry, colorwash the wall inside the frame in the Cantaloupe Glaze to add depth and create the panel.

4 Initials painted freehand in Bubblegum Pink Glaze add a whimsical, decorative touch between the two windows. The monogram panel is painted about 6" (15 cm) below the ceiling.

featured colors for bathroom

- Pink latex eggshell basecoat
- Sunny's Goodtime Raspberry Glaze combination color for the wall finish*
- Yellow-gold latex eggshell for the star stencil

*Note: To create Sunny's Goodtime Raspberry Glaze, mix 4 oz. Sunny's Goodtime Original Antique Aging Glaze with 20 oz. Sunny's Goodtime Ruby Red Glaze.

A princess-y panel on Cantaloupe glazed walls.

A bath fit for a princess.

In the bathroom, the pink basecoat with a Raspberry glaze is offset by a bright yellow star in latex paint.

GENERAL INSTRUCTIONS FOR THE BATHROOM

1 Paint the walls in pink. Let them dry for at least 5 days.

2 Colorwash the wall with Raspberry Glaze and allow to dry for approximately 20 minutes.

3 Create a star stencil and make chalk marks for stencil positioning. (See Monogram Me! project on page 37 for how to stencil.)

4 Stencil the stars with yellow-gold paint.

gone fishin'

TECHNIQUES

freehand

featured colors

- **Light sky blue latex eggshell basecoat**
- **Various acrylic paints for the fishing lures**
- **Dark gray acrylic tube paint for the fishing line**

FOR A BOY WHO'S WILD ABOUT FISHING, I couldn't resist a border of fishing line and lures. The walls and the ceiling are blue. The freehand border is inspired in part by an antique buoy, a folkloric piece that now adorns the closet door. I sketched the art on paper, in keeping with the rustic quality of the buoy, using a simple design that was relatively easy to transfer onto the walls.

Think about how this same idea might work for a girl who loves flowers (see flower vine border on page 80), a boy who adores cars, or an older girl who dreams of shoes. No need to compete with Michelangelo—a few simple drawings add originality and character to any child's room.

A weathered fishing buoy suggested the theme.

far right: Closeup of a painted fish lure in the border.

GENERAL INSTRUCTIONS

1 Paint the wall in sky blue for the basecoat and let dry for at least 5 days.

2 Sketch out the planned decorations in chalk around the upper edge of the room, on as many walls as you want.

3 Do a few test paintings on paper for models of the lures; then paint the lures freehand on the walls at well-spaced intervals in acrylic paint. Keep your paint fairly dry so it does not run.

Mix and match

The same border would look great on a pale green, light gray, or tan wall. Get color ideas for the border from actual fly fishing lures, which are works of art themselves.

The finished room with whimsical painted border.

flights of fancy

TECHNIQUES

freehand, stencil

USING A SIMPLE YET LOVELY monogrammed plaque as the jumping-off point, I gave this room a cherished and wholly original new look. Lovebirds stenciled on in gold with freehand wisps match the delicate, old-fashioned patterns on the plaque and on the painted furniture. I love using this pattern about a third of the way down from the ceiling, because it makes the room cozier.

featured colors

- **Light pink latex eggshell for the basecoat**
- **Tan acrylic eggshell paint for the bird stencil and wisps**

opposite: Wispy freehand swirls add feminine details.

right: A wooden plaque inspired the decorative accents created with paint.

Lovebird stencils enchant and inspire.

GENERAL INSTRUCTIONS

1 Paint the walls in the basecoat. Let them dry for at least 5 days.

2 Make a horizontal line around the upper part of walls where you want stenciling and decoration.

3 Make chalk marks for stencil positioning. (See Monogram Me! project on page 37 for how to stencil.)

4 Get or make a bird stencil. (The stencil shown here is one of Sunny's.) Sketch loop designs around walls in chalk to connect the birds.

5 Stencil birds using tan paint. Connect the bird stencils freehand using a thin artist's paintbrush and tan paint.

little boy blue

featured colors

- **Off-white (with a blue tint) latex eggshell basecoat**
- **Light purple-blue latex eggshell**

BLUE MAY BE FOR BOYS ACCORDING to tradition, but there's nothing conventional about this little boy's blue room. Hand-stitched quilts in blue and fire-engine red inspired the pale blue gingham-patterned walls. The subtle shadings in the checkerboard pattern add dimension and light to the small space and coexist beautifully with the bold fabrics and painted furnishings.

GENERAL INSTRUCTIONS

First paint the walls the base color and let them dry for at least 5 days.

INSTRUCTIONS FOR CHECKERBOARD

Marking the Vertical Stripes

1 Measure 12" (30.5 cm) from the corner, and mark the a short vertical line on the wall with chalk.

2 Continue marking the wall, measuring 12" (30.5 cm) between each mark.

3 If the last stripe is too wide or too narrow, offset the irreg-

The quilt design inspired the room color and pattern.

ular width by combining the width of the last stripe and the stripe beside it, dividing that total in half, and using one-half of the total width for each stripe. Once the room is complete, you won't notice the off-size width.

4 Using the level, draw the vertical lines with chalk all along the wall, at the chalk marks.

Dividing the Stripes Into Boxes

1 Begin in the corner. Starting at the ceiling, measure down 12" (30.5 cm) and mark a line horizontally across with chalk.

2 Continue measuring and marking until you reach about 12" (30.5 cm) from the bottom of the wall.

3 Using the level, draw the lines with chalk horizontally across the wall at the marks. You now have drawn squares.

Taping Off and Painting the Checkerboard

1 Using brown paper tape, tape around the first few checkerboard squares you plan to paint at the top of the wall. You are taping off every other square to create the pattern (see photo opposite for pattern).

2 Place a small section of brown tape on the squares that are not being painted to help you remember which areas to skip.

3 Apply the paint with a brush in the center of the square working out to the tape edges.

4 Pull off the brown tape after a few squares have been painted.

5 Continue taping off and painting every other square until your checkerboard pattern is complete.

The completed checkerboard patterned wall.

be mine, flower vine

TECHNIQUES

colorwash, freehand

featured colors:

- **Light green latex eggshell basecoat**
- **Sunny's Goodtime Avocado Colour Wash combination color below the border***
- **Sunny's Goodtime Apricot Colour Wash**
- **Pink, yellow, and red latex paint for the flowers (acrylic tube paints could be used also)**
- **Green latex paint for the leaves and vines**

*Note: To create Sunny's Goodtime Avocado Colour Wash, mix 12 oz. Sunny's Goodtime Lizard Lime Colour Wash with 12 oz. Sunny's Goodtime Gator Green Glaze.

THE NEAT HAND-STITCHING ON THIS QUILT and the gerbera daisy pattern inspired a charming flower vine border in this girl's room. The vine pattern mimics the quilt stitches, looping around the room and dancing across the top of the mirror. Believe it or not, the stitches are easier to paint than a fluid line. The border is painted just above crib height, so the baby will have lots to see as she starts to pull herself up. The pink, yellow, and orange flowers are chalked on the wall and then painted freehand. The vine pattern also makes a wonderful growth chart.

right: Quilted flowers inspired the overall theme and room colors.

opposite: An avocado wash below the border saturates the room with color.

The vine design creates a lovely accent around the bureau and mirror.

INSTRUCTIONS FOR FREEHAND VINE

1 Paint the walls in green latex eggshell and let dry for at least 5 days.

2 Use chalk to outline the horizontal vine pattern. I used green chalk to match the green paint (Photo 1).

3 Glaze the area of the wall beneath where the horizontal vines are drawn; let the glaze dry for 4 hours. Glazing is very much like colorwash, so see Marching Elephants project on page 31 for how-to details.

4 Use chalk to mark any remaining vines to be drawn.

5 I used a #4 artist's brush to apply the green latex paint freehand for the vines (Photo 2).

Photo 1. Sketch the vine pattern outline with chalk.

Photo 2. Use an artist's brush to apply the paint for the vines.

A vine growth chart near the door adds a playful element to the room.

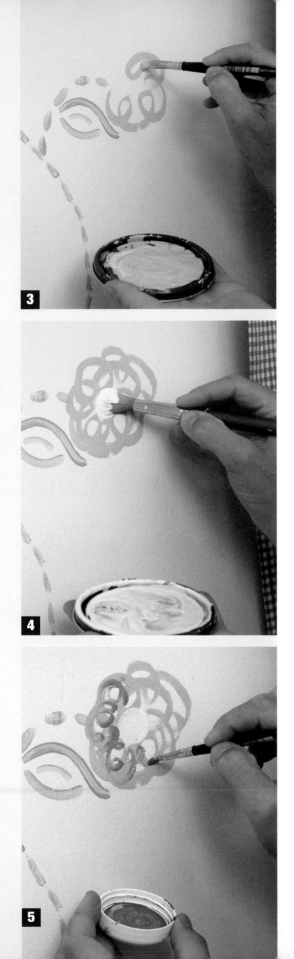

6 This flower pattern is so easy—it's almost a doodle. Use green for the leaves and vine, pink for the petals (Photo 3). Apricot colorwash was added to the paint, to give it more of a watercolor feel, looser and more whimsical.

7 Be creative! Use some petal color to shade in the leaves or a spot of yellow at each flower's center (Photo 4).

8 Finish each flower with a contrasting color. I used #2 and #4 artist's brushes for the pink and orange flourishes. You want the flowers to appear hand-painted, not to look like wallpaper, so mix them up. Use different finishing shades and different brush sizes to vary the look among the petals (Photo 5).

9 A finished flower is shown opposite.

Photo 3. Easy freehand petals, practically doodling.

Photo 4. Bright yellow centers.

Photo 5. Mix and match the petal colors for contrast.

The freehand flower vine mimics
the hand-stitched quilt.

The border, slightly higher than
crib height, gives the baby
something to see.

buckin' bronco

TECHNIQUES

aging glaze, freehand border, stencil

featured colors

- Off-white (with a yellow tint) latex eggshell basecoat
- Sunny's Goodtime Original Antique Aging Glaze for below the border
- Dark red latex eggshell for the scalloped border
- Medium brown latex eggshell for the boot stencil

THESE BOOTS WERE MADE FOR STENCILIN'! The walls in this room were finished below the border with an aging glaze. Note that the deep red scalloped border climbs onto the ceiling, a visual that works especially well in this irregularly shaped room. The boot stencil was inspired by the child's own cowboy boots. He'll outgrow the shoes long before he outgrows the room. Chalkboards or bulletin boards can easily be added to the room, along with an array of school art and photographs.

right: A child's cowboy boots inspired the stencil.

opposite: The red border picks up the color and feeling of other cowboy-themed decorations and toys in the room.

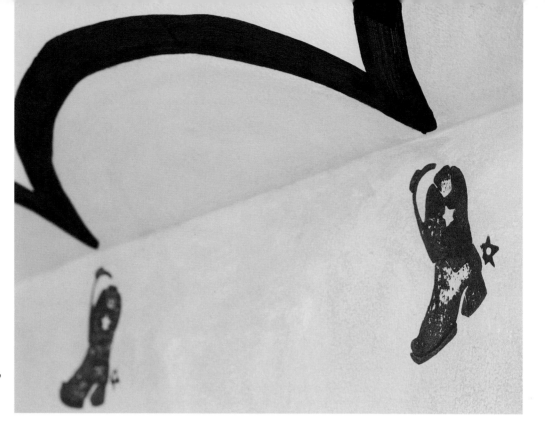

Closeup of red scallops, painted freehand, and stenciled boots.

GENERAL INSTRUCTIONS

1 Paint the walls with the off-white latex eggshell basecoat. Let dry for at least 5 days.

2 Apply the aging glaze to the walls only by brushing it on with a wide paintbrush and rubbing it with a clean rag, as if you were washing your windows. Let the glaze dry for 4 hours.

3 Here's where your ladder will come in handy. Measure the width of the wall at the ceiling and divide it with chalk tick marks into equal segments, about 12" (30 cm) wide.

4 With chalk draw freehand scallop designs on the ceiling, starting at one tick mark and ending at the next. If necessary, add a horizontal line at the top of the scallops in chalk for guidance.

5 Using a 1" (2.5 cm) wide artist's paintbrush and dark red latex eggshell paint, paint the scallops around the ceiling (see photos).

6 Make a boot stencil. Use a sponge and the medium brown paint to stencil in the boot pattern at the point of each scallop. Use red paint for the spurs.

rugby stripe

TECHNIQUES

horizontal stripe, pinstripe

featured colors

- **Pale blue latex eggshell basecoat**
- **Sunny's Goodtime Marine Glaze for the wash**
- **Green latex eggshell for the green pinstripe**

THERE MAY BE MORE to your child's laundry than meets the eye. A favorite article of clothing just might translate into an inspired room design. The stripes on a rugby shirt, for example, were the inspiration for this wall's horizontal stripe. The clean stripe works with any number of fabric and room themes. A simple stripe unifies the space and adds structure and a punch of color. A mask the child made in art class adds a personal touch to this room (see next page).

A favorite shirt inspired the striped border in this boy's room.

GENERAL INSTRUCTIONS

1 Paint the walls in a pale blue basecoat. Let them dry for at least 5 days.

2 Use a level to draw a horizontal line with chalk 12" (30.5 cm) down from the ceiling all around the room on the walls you want to stripe.

3 Mark 12" (30.5 cm) down from the first line with chalk and draw it all around the room on the walls you want to stripe.

4 Apply a strip of 2" (5 cm) brown paper tape along the top and bottom of the two chalk lines to protect the wall when glazing.

5 Apply the Marine Glaze with a 2" (5 cm) natural bristle brush between the pieces of tape and blend with a clean rag.

6 After the glaze has dried (about 20 minutes), tape off the pinstripes above and below the glazed band: align the outside of the pinstripe tape ¼" (6 mm) from the top or bottom of the 2" (5 cm) brown tape.

7 Use a narrow artist's brush to apply the green latex eggshell paint for the pinstripe.

8 Remove the tape when the paint is dry.

Mix and match

For the same stripe in orange with a green pinstripe on green walls:

- Yellow-gold latex eggshell basecoat
- Sunny's Goodtime Apricot Colour Wash for the 12" (30.5 cm) stripe
- Green latex eggshell for the ¼" (6 mm) stripe

Finished room with its rugby shirt border.

Marine Glaze stripe with green pinstripe.

Apricot wash stripe with green pinstripe.

"Grab hold and let your **imagination soar!**"

ages 9 through 12

rooms to think and dream in

cotton candy stripes

TECHNIQUES

colorwash, stripes

featured colors

- **White latex eggshell basecoat**
- **Sunny's Goodtime Bubblegum Pink Colour Wash combination color for the stripes***

   *Note: To create Sunny's Goodtime Bubblegum Pink, mix 16 oz. Sunny's Goodtime Palm Beach Pink Colour Wash with 8 oz. Sunny's Goodtime Ruby Red Glaze.

THE VIBRANT COLORS IN A bandana-print fabric are counterbalanced by soft pink stripes in this girl's room. The stripes are 12" (30.5 cm) swaths of hot pink colorwash and white, which are accented by hot pink lampshades and bright green and white furnishings. Solid pink walls wouldn't have the same flair as these cotton-candy stripes. When you want a change, add a white stencil to the middle of the pink stripe or add pinstripes in a darker pink or green.

GENERAL INSTRUCTIONS

1 Paint walls in white latex basecoat. Let dry for at least 5 days.

2 Measure stripes and tape off walls (see Peppy Preppy project on page 55).

3 Glaze alternate stripes with Bubblegum Pink glaze; let dry and remove tape.

right: A bandana print quilt inspired the room colors.

opposite: Bubblegum Pink stripes.

Pale pink stripes bring disparate elements of the room together.

Mix and match

For a pink stripe with a green pinstripe:

- Pale pink latex eggshell basecoat

- Sunny's Goodtime Bubblegum Pink Colour Wash combination color for the 12" (30.5 cm) stripe*

- Avocado green latex eggshell for the 1/4" (6 mm) stripe

  *Note: To create Sunny's Goodtime Bubblegum Pink Colour Wash, mix 16 oz. Sunny's Goodtime Palm Beach Pink Colour Wash with 8 oz. Sunny's Goodtime Ruby Red Glaze.

The same 12" (30.5 cm) wide stripe in pink with a green pinstripe is another choice (for how-to of pinstripes, see pages 51 to 52).

log cabin

TECHNIQUES

log cabin pattern

featured colors

- Off-white (with a yellow tint) latex eggshell basecoat
- Sunny's Goodtime Cappuccino Glaze for the log cabin pattern

HORIZONTAL STRIPES IN BEIGE AND CREAM create a log cabin atmosphere in this boy's room. For a boy who loves nature, the subtle, neutral colors work with a range of fabrics and will take him from toddler to teen.

Stripes painted on with a 2" (5 cm) brush create a striated effect.

Nature inspired the color.

This pattern works for toddlers or teens.

INSTRUCTIONS FOR LOG CABIN

1 Paint the walls in the basecoat color.

2 Begin by measuring down 17" (43.2 cm) from the ceiling. This marks the first log. Make a horizontal line with your level and chalk.

3 Measure down 3" (7.5 cm) from that line and make another horizontal line. The space between the lines is your mortar.

4 Repeat marking lines at 17" (43.2 cm) and 3" (7.5 cm) intervals until you reach the bottom of the wall.

5 Continue around the room, marking all four walls, or as many as you want to paint.

opposite: Horizontal stripes evoke the feel of a log cabin.

6 Tape off log lines with brown painter's tape. The mortar line will be underneath the tape and will be protected from paint.

7 Apply the glaze to the center of the horizontal stripe with a 2" (5 cm) natural bristle brush. Brush sideways (horizontally), leaving the top and bottom sections of the stripe for last, when there's the least amount of glaze on your brush.

8 Logs will look more natural if you apply the glaze with a brush and leave it alone. Do not rub the glaze in with a cloth. The more irregular the strokes, the more natural the wood grain looks.

mermaid's bower

TECHNIQUES

colorwash, freehand border, dot stencil

featured colors

- White latex eggshell basecoat
- Sunny's Goodtime Marine Glaze for the wash and swirl pattern
- Lime green latex eggshell paint for the dots

A FAVORITE MERMAID PILLOW and decorative fabrics inspired the mermaid theme and tonal blues in this girl's room. The 10' (3 m)-high ceilings called for a border that was deep and in keeping with the majestic scale of the room. I used the swirl pattern from the drapes and bedding to create the green dots and blue whirls and eddies of the border. The swirl pattern repeats on architectural details elsewhere in the room, and the lime-green dot stencils continue the theme on the wall above the desk. The large-scale swirl adds atmosphere; the border at half its size would make no impact. The mermaid theme is also carried out in all the nooks and crannies of the room, but it doesn't overpower.

right: Fabric patterns inspired the scroll border.

opposite: A mermaid doll inspired an aquatic theme.

Closeup of the Marine Glaze patterned border with Lime Green dots.

GENERAL INSTRUCTIONS

1 Paint base color on walls; let them dry for at least 5 days.

2 Use the Marine Glaze for a wash over the walls. Let dry for 20 minutes.

3 Draw the swirl patterns in chalk. Adjust if needed to fill the spaces well.

4 Using a small artist's paintbrush and Marine Glaze, paint on the swirl patterns.

5 After the swirls have dried, use a dot stencil and the lime green paint for the dot patterns.

left: Extend the border to all of the architectural details in the room for the most dramatic effect.

below: The lime dots carry over to the wall above the desk.

sticks and stripes

TECHNIQUES

horizontal stripes, colorwash

featured colors

- **Light khaki latex eggshell basecoat and for the 2" (5 cm) and 6" (15 cm) stripes**
- **Sunny's Goodtime Original Antique Aging Glaze for the 14" (35.6 cm) stripe**
- **Medium tan latex eggshell for the ¼" (6 mm) and 2" (5 cm) stripes**
- **Sunny's Goodtime Apricot Colour Wash for the 5½" (14 cm) stripe**
- **Sunny's Goodtime French Gray Colour Wash for the 3" (7.5 cm) and 6" (15 cm) stripes**
- **Sunny's Goodtime Fern Glaze combination color for the 1" (2.5 cm) inch stripe***
- **Sunny's Goodtime Apricot Colour Wash for the ¾" (1.9 cm) stripe**
- **Medium purple latex eggshell for the ¼" (6 mm) stripe**

*To make the Fern Glaze combination color, combine Sunny's Gator Green Glaze and Original Glaze.

PAINTING A SINGLE WALL can make a big statement in a room, especially if the wall is striped. Here we chose the largest wall that had no windows or doors.

The bold multicolor stripes in a rug inspired the horizontal stripes painted on the accent wall. Greens, blues, yellows, and browns alternate with khaki and white to create stripes of varying widths across the wall. First, the entire wall was painted a light khaki. The 2" and 6" wide (5 cm and 15 cm) stripes are the base khaki color. I marked the wall off in 14" (35.6 cm) horizontal stripes and added varying widths to every other stripe for interest.

right: The multicolor stripes in this rug inspired the wall pattern.

opposite: A focal point wall of stripes.

Varying widths and pinstripes for accent.

INSTRUCTIONS FOR HORIZONTAL STRIPES

1 Measure the stripes from the top of the wall down.

2 The more random widths and colors you have, the better. Try not to make them even.

3 Always glaze the top stripe first.

4 Let each stripe dry before you do the next one.

catch a wave

TECHNIQUES
colorwash, freehand

featured colors

- **Pale blue latex eggshell basecoat**
- **Sunny's Goodtime Marine Glaze** for below the wave border

FUN, FUN, FUN. With a little imagination, some blue glaze, and a paintbrush, the surf can always be up. A freehand blue wave creates a reverse canopy in this surf-inspired boy's room. The walls were colorwashed in marine blue. The wave drawing was sketched onto the wall with blue chalk before the details were painted on with an artist's brush. I used a rag to apply the colorwash beneath the wave pattern. By making the wave come three-quarters of the way up the wall, we created depth around the room.

above: Wave pattern in Marine Glaze.

right: A quilt square inspired the color and theme.

INSTRUCTIONS
FOR FREEHAND WAVE

1 Paint the walls with the pale blue latex basecoat.
Let them dry for at least 5 days.

2 Use colored chalk to draw the outline of the wave onto
the wall. The top of this border is 16" (40.6 cm) from
the ceiling (Photo 1).

3 Once the wave outline is complete, apply the Marine
Glaze using a 2" (5 cm) natural bristle brush (Photo 2).

4 Use a cotton rag to blend in the glaze as you apply it,
alternating brush and rag to get the desired colorwash
effect (Photo 3).

Photo 1. Use colored chalk to sketch the
wave pattern onto the wall.

Photo 2. Apply paint using a 2" (5 cm)
natural bristle brush.

Photo 3. Use a cotton rag to blend in the
colorwash as you apply the paint with
the brush.

opposite: Create a reverse canopy with
a freehand blue wave border.

Closeup of freehand wave
in Marine Glaze in corner.

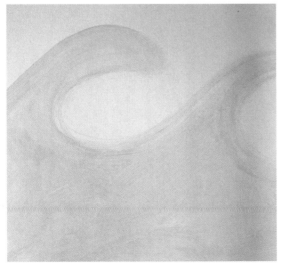

An alternative color for the wave is Bahama Blue
Colour Wash.

Mix and match

The wave pattern also works nicely in a different shade
of blue.

- White latex eggshell basecoat
- Sunny's Goodtime Bahama Blue Colour Wash
  for below the wave border

painted headboard

TECHNIQUE

freehand

featured colors

- **Pale yellow latex eggshell basecoat**
- **Light blue latex eggshell for the headboard**

ONE OF THE EASIEST WAYS TO ADD a decorative flourish to any bedroom is to paint a headboard for the bed. Whimsical and colorful, and much less expensive than a new bed! In this room, once the decision was made to paint a head-board, the whole project was completed in only an hour. We chose blue to echo the pinstripe of the bed linens.

Your design can be as simple as this or more elaborate. Use fabric for inspiration and sketch headboards to your heart's content until you find a shape that's just right.

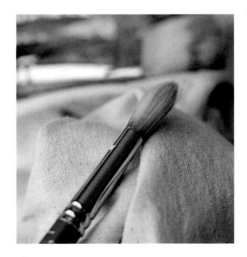

above: You'll need a thin artist's brush to paint the outlines.

right: The pinstripe in the bed linens inspired the color choice for the headboard.

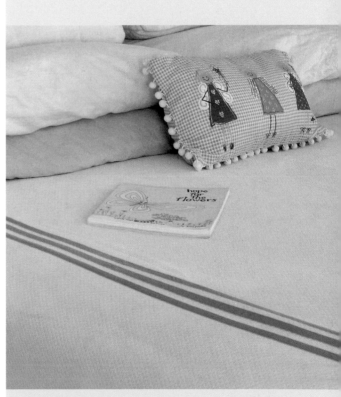

INSTRUCTIONS FOR PAINTED HEADBOARD

1 Paint the walls with the yellow latex eggshell paint. Let dry for at least 5 days.

2 Measure the start and width of the headboard by marking on the wall in chalk where the top of the mattress hits the wall at each side. I usually allow about the width of the bed for the width of the headboard, which may vary, depending on the shape and the drama I intend to create. Measure off about 2' to 3½' (61 cm to 1.1 m) from the top of the mattress to get the height of painted headboard (Photo 1).

3 The very simple design shown was sketched on the wall first with blue colored chalk before painting. (Remember to move the bed out of the way before you sketch or paint!)

4 Paint the outlines with a thin artist's brush and then fill in (Photos 2 and 3).

5 Use a wider brush for filling in.

Photo 1. Measure the width of the bed to approximate your headboard's width, and measure up a few feet to sketch out the headboard shape in chalk.

Photos 2 and 3. When your design is sketched completely and looks the way you want it to look, use an artist's brush to apply paint. Paint the outside lines first and then paint inside those lines, as they tell you to do in school.

opposite: A painted headboard gives definition to a room, and it's easy to do.

at home in the castle

TECHNIQUE

stoneblock

featured colors

- **Off-white (with a yellow tint) latex eggshell basecoat**
- **Sunny's Goodtime Original Antique Aging Glaze for the stoneblock pattern**

FAUX STONEBLOCKS LEND A MEDIEVAL AIR to this boy's room. The pattern works well with a wild boar, horseshoes, and any other rugged treasures you find in a ten-year-old boy's room.

The basic concept of stoneblock is simple. Walls are painted an off-white color and allowed to dry for at least 5 days. Rectangles imitating large stoneblocks are marked on the walls you want to decorate, starting from the top down. Then the outlines of the rectangles are protected by thin tape while a stone-colored glaze is rubbed on. When the tape is removed, the unpainted areas simulate the mortar that holds real stoneblocks together.

opposite: A stoneblock pattern gives this room a medieval flair.

The stoneblock effect was created with an off-white basecoat and aging glaze.

INSTRUCTIONS FOR STONEBLOCK

Marking the Horizontal Lines

1 Start in an inconspicuous corner. Measure 12" (30.5 cm) down from the line where the ceiling meets a wall, and mark the 12" (30.5 cm) distance with a chalk dot.

2 Using the level, continue measuring and marking 12" (30.5 cm) down from the ceiling line around any walls you plan to do in stoneblock.

3 Using the level, draw a horizontal line to connect the row of chalk marks you just made 12" (30.5 cm) down, all around the room. The horizontal lines should align at each corner. In Photo 1 the top round of stoneblocks already has been marked, taped, and glazed, and the author is measuring the second round (Photo 1).

4 Continue measuring downwards and marking 12" (30.5 cm) distances between horizontal lines. Then use the level to connect the chalk marks. Draw all the horizontal lines needed to fill your wall.

Marking the Vertical Lines for Stoneblock

1 Measure around the top horizontal line and mark chalk dots at 24" (61 cm) intervals.

2 Draw vertical lines from the chalk dots you just made down to the next horizontal chalk line (Photo 2). Each block will be 24" (61 cm) wide and 12" (30.5 cm) deep.

Photo 1. At top, one round of stoneblocks is already marked and glazed. Draw a horizontal line around the room 12" (30.5 cm) down from the previous line, using the level.

Photo 2. Draw the vertical marks at 24" (61 cm) intervals to mark a row of blocks all around the room.

3 For the second row of blocks, start 12" (30.5 cm) in from the side edge of the block above it and mark a vertical line. Then measure horizontally 24" (61 cm) to mark the next vertical line. Skipping the first 12" on the horizontal line means that the blocks will align in a staggered pattern (see Photo 8 for example). Continue measuring horizontally and marking dots with chalk at 24" (61 cm) intervals around the room on the second row.

4 Draw vertical lines where the chalk dots are around the second row.

5 For the remaining rows, mark lines as before, spacing new vertical lines 12" (30.5 cm) away from the previous line in the column. Use the vertical lines from the first row as references in order to space the lines for the third row, and so on.

6 If the stoneblock at the end of the row is too big or too small, add the last block's width and the width of the previous block and divide the result in two to make two narrower-than-usual or two wider-than-usual blocks of equal width.

Taping Off the Lines before Glazing

1 First tape off all the horizontal lines with the white artist's tape (Photo 3), and then tape all the vertical lines (Photo 4).

2 Use 1" (2.5 cm) wide blue painter's tape on any moldings and baseboards to protect them.

Photo 3. Cover the horizontal chalk lines with thin white artist's tape. The taped areas remain unglazed.

Photo 4. Cover all the vertical lines with artist's tape too.

Glazing

1 Brush the glaze on and rub it with a rag as though you were cleaning the walls. Use a colorwash or an aging glaze tinted a neutral color like off-white or beige, depending on the room (Photos 5 and 6).

2 Remove the tape promptly after painting (Photo 7)

3 Using a rag, carefully remove any paint that may have seeped under the tape (Photo 8).

4 The line that the artist's tape covered looks like the mortar between the blocks when the tape is removed.

tip

To keep the glaze from bleeding under the tape, apply it to the center of each block and rub out to the edge, glazing one block at a time. Remove the tape promptly.

Photo 5. Apply the glaze with a brush and rub it in with a rag.

Photo 6. Continue to apply the glaze and rub it in.

Photo 7. Remove the tape promptly after glazing.

Photo 8. With a rag, carefully remove any excess paint that seeped under the tape.

garden girl

TECHNIQUES

freehand, colorwash

featured colors

- **Pale pink latex eggshell basecoat**
- **Sunny's Goodtime Grass Glaze combination color and Sunny's Goodtime Avocado Colour Wash combination color for the vines***
- **Red-orange latex eggshell for the flowers**

*Note: To create Sunny's Goodtime Grass Glaze, mix 8 oz. Sunny's Goodtime Gator Green Glaze with 16 oz. Sunny's Goodtime Sunshine Daydream Glaze. To create Sunny's Goodtime Avocado Colour Wash, mix 12 oz. Sunny's Goodtime Lizard Lime Colour Wash with 12 oz. Sunny's Goodtime Gator Green Glaze.

A GIRL'S ROOM IS NOT ONLY HER SANCTUARY from the world, it may also be the place where she dreams of other worlds. And what better place to dream than in a garden? The walled garden theme here is inspired by the gorgeous toile fabric on the pelmet and canopy. The idea with paint is to echo the images of the gazebo and garden wall with easy brush strokes on the wall. You don't have to replicate the details of the image, just try to create the mood and idea of the print.

The simple edging with freehand flower vines adds a romantic touch she'll adore into her teens. It's also nice to take the vine up onto the ceiling every now and again.

The gazebo in the drapery fabric inspired the garden wall theme.

INSTRUCTIONS FOR FREEHAND DESIGNS

1 Paint the walls with the pale pink base color and let dry for at least 5 days.

2 Draw the vines and trellis in chalk; use ruler to get lines straight for trellis. Sketch in vines and leaves freehand.

3 Use Avocado Colour Wash and a narrow artist's paintbrush to do trellis and leaves. (See Be Mine, Flower Vine, for freehand demonstration.)

4 When vines and trellis are dry, paint in flowers in red.

5 Sketch the monogram circle in chalk and paint it and the initials in red.

above: A monogram imitates the toile pattern.

opposite: A dreamy bedroom.

The garden wall is easily sketched onto the wall and accented with freehand flowers.

grandmother's house

TECHNIQUE

colorwash

featured colors

- **Off-white (with a yellow tint) latex eggshell basecoat**
- **Sunny's Goodtime Bahama Blue Colour Wash**

THE THIRD FLOOR OF THIS WEEKEND river house is devoted to grandchildren. The fabric of the drapes inspired the blue colorwash, which is perhaps the simplest decorative painting technique to learn, and the perfect solution for easy decorating in the grandchildren's rooms. You can see colorwash technique instructions in the Marching Elephants project. The wash can create whimsy or sophistication. Here we went for a whimsical blue, taking our cue from the cabanas on the window treatment.

opposite: Blue colorwash enlivens a room in grandmother's house.

right: The colors in the drapes inspired the wash.

Sunshine Daydream Glaze brings in the sun for an alternate color.

INSTRUCTIONS FOR COLORWASH

1 Apply Bahama Blue wash to clean wall with 2" (5 cm) natural bristle brush.

2 Use a clean white cotton rag to blend the product to the desired colorwash effect.

Mix and match

Yellow or pink colorwashed walls would also work well in this room:

- For yellow, use an off-white (with a yellow tint) latex eggshell basecoat and Sunny's Goodtime Sunshine Daydream Glaze

- For pink, use an off-white (with a yellow tint) latex eggshell basecoat and Sunny's Goodtime Bubblegum Pink Colour Wash combination color*

  *Note: To create Sunny's Goodtime Bubblegum Pink, mix 16 oz Sunny's Goodtime Palm Beach Pink Colour Wash with 8 oz. Sunny's Goodtime Ruby Red Glaze.

Bubblegum Pink works in this room too.

up, up, and away!

TECHNIQUES

glaze, freehand, chalkboard

featured colors

- Tan latex eggshell for the basecoat
- Sunny's Goodtime Original Antique Aging Glaze for below the border
- Medium yellow and medium tan for the rope border
- Custom chalkboard paint: mix 32 oz. of medium gray-brown latex flat with 16 oz. Sunny's Goodtime Clear Glaze and 8 oz. of unsanded tile grout
- Dark red and brick red latex eggshell for the chalkboard border tassels

ANY TOY OR BELOVED *OBJECT D'ART* can become the inspiration for your room design. The vent lines on a whimsical papier maché balloon were the inspiration for the unexpected freehand rope border around this boy's room. Grab hold and let your imagination soar!

The wall is glazed below the border, adding depth and color saturation to the wall. This treatment typically requires no ladder. We literally walked around the room and drew a wavy line with chalk, which became the rope border.

The chalkboard trimmed in red adds a practical element and makes coming down to earth fun, too.

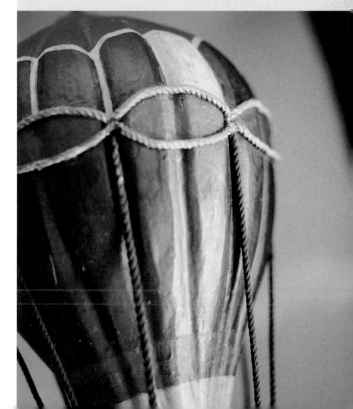

A hot-air balloon decoration was the inspiration for the room's theme.

INSTRUCTIONS FOR CHALKBOARD

A chalkboard doesn't have to be square or black! You control the design and the color—so create a board that's unique to your child's room. I made an irregularly shaped, chocolate brown board here to blend in with the wall color and rope border.

1 Paint the room in the basecoat color. Let it dry for 5 days.

2 Sketch the outline of your chalkboard border on the wall with chalk.

3 Paint the border outline with chalkboard paint (Photo 1).

4 Roll the chalkboard paint onto the wall inside the border. I recommend two or three coats, letting the paint dry between coats (Photo 2).

5 Once the base is dry, use chalk to sketch the border (Photo 3).

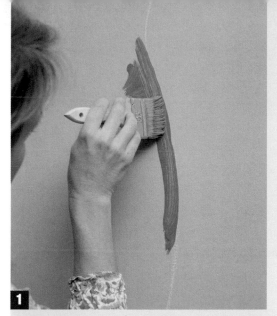

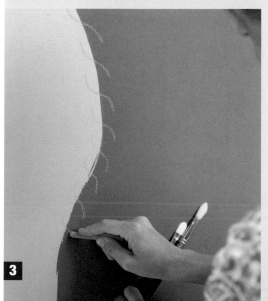

Photo 1. After the chalkboard shape is sketched in chalk, paint along the chalk border to create the chalkboard form.

Photo 2. Roll the chalkboard paint onto the wall for the big areas. Use two or three coats.

Photo 3. Sketch the rope border once the basecoat of paint is dry.

opposite: A fanciful rope border enlivens the room.

6 Use a #12 round synthetic artist's brush to apply the border paint (Photo 4).

7 Next, apply the second paint color, here a dark red, to the border (Photo 5).

8 Let the chalkboard and border dry for 48 hours; then condition the board by rubbing the side of a piece of chalk all over the surface and wiping it off. This creates a barrier between the paint and the writing surface so that the chalkboard will be erasable. Do not use chalkboard pens, as they are not erasable on painted chalk surfaces (Photo 6).

Mix and match

Alternative chalkboard design—this time it's a tent!

- Pale pink latex eggshell basecoat
- Medium purple-blue for the tent
- Black chalkboard paint

Photo 4. Use a #12 round synthetic artist's brush to apply red paint on alternate rope twists.

Photo 5. Apply the second paint color around the edge of the chalkboard form in the spaces skipped earlier.

Photo 6. Condition the chalkboard by rubbing the side of a piece of chalk over the completely dry surface.

Chalkboards can be designed in other styles also, like this one, which imitates a tent.

The chalkboard is a focal point in the room and lots of fun, too.

knot knot

TECHNIQUE

freehand

featured colors

- **Light blue latex eggshell basecoat**
- **Light tan and white latex eggshell for the sailing knot**

A NAUTICAL THEME SEEMED THE natural way to go for these teak bunk beds—especially since the family has been in the yacht-building business for generations. The pale blue walls are embellished with a tan and white knot painted above the built-in dresser. This is actually a sheet bend knot, which is similar to a square knot. The book of sailing knots that inspired this design says it's easy to tie this particular knot. I say it's even easier to paint one!

GENERAL INSTRUCTIONS

1 Paint the walls with the basecoat color. Let them dry for at least 5 days.

2 Create the sailing knot drawings in chalk.

3 Paint the rope in freehand with white paint. See chalkboard demo in Up, Up, and Away! for how to paint rope, but use light tan and white paint instead.

right: A sheet bend sailing knot created with paint.

opposite: The knots extend the other nautical themes in the room.

glossary of paint terms

aging glaze: a glaze applied to walls, furniture, or floors to give the appearance of age.

bristles: the working part of a brush, which may be natural (usually hog hair) or artificial (nylon or polyester).

clearcoat: a transparent protective and/or decorative film.

colorwash: a thin, high-pigment water-based paint that is made to be applied by literally washing your walls; it gives a watery fresco effect.

durability: the ability of paint to last or hold up well upon exposure to destructive agents such as weather, sunlight, detergents, abrasion, and marring.

eggshell: the degree of gloss between flat and semi-gloss finish.

enamel: a broad classification of paints that dry to a hard finish; they may be flat, semi-gloss, or high-gloss and can be water- or oil-based.

exterior: the outside surfaces of a structure.

fading: the loss of color caused by exposure to light, heat, and weathering.

flat: a paint surface that scatters or absorbs the light falling on it so as to be substantially free from gloss or sheen.

glaze: a transparent, often tinted finish, applied over a painted surface to add the illusion of texture, create interest, or soften the original color.

gloss: the luster or shininess of paints and coatings.

grout: a mixture of cement and water or cement, sand, and water used to fill cracks between tiles or other masonry. Use nonsanded grout to prepare chalkboard paint mixture.

interior: the inside surfaces of a structure.

latex-based paint: a general term for water-based emulsion paint, such as polyvinyl acetate, styrene butadiene, and acrylic.

metallics: a class of paints that include metal flakes in their composition.

oil-based paints: those made with drying oil and mineral spirits or paint thinner; they generally dry very hard but take longer to dry than latex paints and require more time to recoat.

pigments: paint ingredients mainly used to impart color and hiding power.

polyacrylic: a water-based protective topcoat, usually non-yellowing; can only be used with water-based paints.

polyurethane: a kind of paint with an oil base; it comes in a wide range of coatings, ranging from hard gloss enamels to soft, flexible ones. Polyurethane takes longer to dry than polyacrylic and yellows with age. It can be used on top of either oil- or- water-based paints.

primer: the first coat or undercoat that helps to bind the topcoat to the substrate; such paints are designed to provide adequate adhesion to new surfaces or are formulated to meet the special requirements of the surfaces.

ragging: a technique for applying glaze to create texture.

semi-gloss: a finish with a low-luster sheen between flat and full gloss.

sheen: the degree of luster of a dried paint film, generally classified as flat, matte, eggshell, semi-gloss, or high-gloss.

shellac: derived from a resinous substance called lac that is formed on certain Asian trees; it is alcohol-based and is used as a sealer and finish for floors, for sealing knots, and for other purposes.

spackle: a powder containing gypsum plaster and glue that when mixed with water forms a paste used to fill cracks and holes in plaster. Spackle is actually a trademark and brand name, but the word is often used as a generic noun or verb.

stippling: tapping a paintbrush lightly and vertically to gain coverage into crevices.

tack: the sticky condition of coating during drying, between the wet and dry-to-touch stages.

texture: the roughness or irregularity of a surface.

undercoat: a primer or intermediate coating before the finish coating.

varnish: a transparent liquid that dries on exposure to air to give a decorative or protective coating when applied as a thin film.

water-based coatings: those in which most of the liquid content is water.

paint specifics for photos

PART 1: ABOUT PAINT

Refer to the individual projects listed below for paint information.

PART 2: NURSERIES FOR WEE ONES (newborn through 3)

marching elephants

Pages 30–31: The wall basecoat is a light blue-gray, Benjamin Moore latex eggshell 875. The elephant is Sunny's Goodtime Little Boy Blue Colour Wash. Various acrylic paints (Anita's All Purpose Acrylic Craft Paint) were used for the elephant stencils and freehand trim. The dot stencils were done in light blue, Benjamin Moore latex eggshell 820. Page 33: **Pink colorwash alternate:** The wall basecoat is Benjamin Moore latex eggshell White. The wash is Sunny's Goodtime Bubblegum Pink Colour Wash combination color (mix 16 oz. Sunny's Goodtime Palm Beach Pink Colour Wash with 8 oz. Sunny's Goodtime Ruby Red Glaze). The elephant is Sunny's French Gray Colour Wash with Anita's All Purpose Acrylic Craft paint in various colors: Lavender, Lily Pad, Tangerine, and Lullabye Blue. Page 33: **Green colorwash alternate:** The wall basecoat is Benjamin Moore latex eggshell White. The wash on the wall is Sunny's Goodtime Lizard Lime Colour Wash. The elephant is Sunny's French Gray Colour Wash with Anita's All Purpose Acrylic Craft Paint in various colors: Lily Pad, Tangerine, and Lavender.

dot, dot, dot

Pages 34–35: **The bedroom:** Wall basecoat is off white, Benjamin Moore latex eggshell 944. The wall finish is Sunny's Goodtime Avocado Colour Wash combination color (mix 12 oz. Sunny's Goodtime Lizard Lime Colour Wash with 12 oz. Sunny's Goodtime Gator Green Glaze). The dots are Sunny's Goodtime Palm Beach Pink Colour Wash. Page 36: **The bathroom:** Wall basecoat is off white, Benjamin Moore latex eggshell 944. The S stencil was done in Sunny's Goodtime Bubblegum Pink Colour Wash (mix 16 oz. Sunny's Goodtime Palm Beach Pink Colour Wash with 8 oz. Sunny's Goodtime Ruby Red Glaze).

monogram me!

Pages 37–39: The wall basecoat is an off-white with a yellow tint, Benjamin Moore latex eggshell Linen White. The walls were washed with Sunny's Goodtime Palm Beach Pink Colour Wash, and the stencil was done in Sunny's Goodtime Bubblegum Pink Colour Wash combination color (mix 16 oz. Sunny's Goodtime Palm Beach Pink Colour Wash with 8 oz. Sunny's Goodtime Ruby Red Glaze). Page 40: **Gold stencil on gray colorwash alternate:** The walls were washed with Sunny's Goodtime French Gray Colour Wash, and the stencil was done in Sunny's metallic gold glaze. Page 40: **Pumpkin stencil on pumpkin colorwash alternate:** The walls were washed with Sunny's Goodtime Pumpkin Glaze, and the stencil was done in the same glaze. Page 40: **Green stencil on green**

colorwash alternate: The walls were washed with Sunny's Goodtime Ocean Age Glaze, and the stencil was done in the same glaze.

lavender's blue

Pages 41–42: The wall basecoat is a pale lavender, Benjamin Moore latex eggshell 2069-70. The walls were washed with Sunny's Goodtime Lavender Colour Wash combination color (mix 12 oz. Sunny's Goodtime La-La Lilac Colour Wash with 12 oz. Sunny's Goodtime Plainly Plum Glaze). Page 43: **Blue colorwash alternate:** The wall basecoat is a medium purple-blue, Benjamin Moore latex eggshell 2067-50. The walls were colorwashed with Sunny's Goodtime Marine Glaze. Page 43: **Green colorwash alternate:** The wall basecoat is a medium lime-green, Benjamin Moore latex eggshell 403. The walls were colorwashed with Sunny's Goodtime Avocado Colour Wash combination color (mix 12 oz. Sunny's Goodtime Lizard Lime Colour Wash with 12 oz. Sunny's Goodtime Gator Green Glaze).

canopy panoply

Pages 44–48: The wall basecoat is off white, Benjamin Moore latex eggshell 944. Below the border is Sunny's Goodtime Palm Beach Pink Colour Wash. The border and dots were done in Sunny's Goodtime Toffee Glaze combination color (mix 10 oz. Original Antique Aging Glaze with 14 oz. Sunny's Goodtime Cappuccino Glaze). Page 48: **White with blue alternate:** The wall basecoat is Benjamin Moore latex eggshell White. The ceiling was washed with Sunny's Goodtime Little Boy Blue Colour Wash. Below the border the wall was washed with Sunny's Goodtime Marine Glaze. The dots were done in a light khaki, Benjamin Moore latex eggshell 1044. The border was painted in a medium beige, Benjamin Moore latex eggshell HC-77. Pages 49-53: **Vertical pinstripes nursery:** The wall basecoat is off white, Benjamin Moore latex eggshell 944. The wide stripes were done with Sunny's Goodtime Toffee Glaze combination color (mix 10 oz. Sunny's Goodtime Original Antique Aging Glaze with 14 oz. Sunny's Goodtime Cappuccino Glaze). The pinstripes were done in chocolate brown (Benjamin Moore latex eggshell HC-76) and pink latex eggshell (Benjamin Moore 1326).

peppy preppy

Pages 54–57: The wall basecoat is a light green, Benjamin Moore latex eggshell 2029-60. The 12" (30.5 cm) stripes were done in Sunny's Goodtime Gator Green Glaze, and Sunny's Goodtime Pumpkin Glaze was used for the scalloped border. The stencils were done in a light rose, Benjamin Moore latex eggshell 1326.

loop-de-loop

Pages 58–61: The wall basecoat is Benjamin Moore latex eggshell White. The walls were colorwashed with Sunny's Goodtime Sunshine Daydream Glaze. The freehand loops were done in

a bright coral, Benjamin Moore latex eggshell 1320, and the dot stencils were painted in a light blue, Benjamin Moore latex eggshell 821.

PART 3: ROOMS TO PLAY AND GROW IN (ages 4 through 8)

creature feature

Pages 64–66: The wall basecoat is a medium yellow-green, Benjamin Moore latex eggshell 412. Sunny's Goodtime Gator Green Glaze was used for the border below the alligators. The alligator stencils were done in a blue custom color combination (mix 4 oz. of a medium purple-blue, Benjamin Moore latex eggshell 2067-50, with 4 oz. Sunny's Goodtime Marine Glaze. Red acrylic tube paint was used for the alligators' eyes. Page 66: Acrylic tube paints in umber and sienna were used for the cattail growth chart.

the royal treatment

Pages 67–69: **The bedroom:** Wall basecoat is pale yellow, Benjamin Moore latex eggshell 2018-60. The scroll was done in Sunny's Goodtime Bubblegum Pink Colour Wash (mix 16 oz. Sunny's Goodtime Palm Beach Pink Colour Wash with 8 oz. Sunny's Goodtime Ruby Red Glaze). The wall was washed with Sunny's Goodtime Cantaloupe Glaze combination color (mix 12 oz. Sunny's Goodtime Pumpkin Glaze with 12 oz. Sunny's Goodtime Sunshine

Daydream Glaze). Page 70: **The bathroom:** Wall basecoat is pink latex eggshell (Benjamin Moore 884). The wall finish is Sunny's Goodtime Raspberry Glaze combination color (mix 4 oz. Sunny's Goodtime Original Antique Aging Glaze with 20 oz. Sunny's Goodtime Ruby Red Glaze). The star stencil was done in a yellow-gold, Benjamin Moore latex eggshell 348.

gone fishin'

Pages 71–72: The wall basecoat is a light sky blue, Benjamin Moore latex eggshell 814. Various acrylic paints were used for the fishing lures. The fishing line is Golden Graphite Gray.

flights of fancy

Pages 74–76: The wall basecoat is a light pink, Benjamin Moore latex eggshell 887. The bird stencil and wisps are a medium beige, Benjamin Moore latex eggshell 1075.

little boy blue

Pages 77–79: The wall basecoat is an off-white (with a blue tint), Benjamin Moore latex eggshell 2067-70. The squares were painted on in a light purple-blue, Benjamin Moore latex eggshell 2067-60.

be mine, flower vine

Pages 80–85: The wall basecoat is avocado green, Benjamin Moore latex eggshell 2029-50. Below the border is Sunny's Goodtime Avocado Colour Wash color combination (mix 12 oz.

Sunny's Goodtime Lizard Lime Colour Wash with 12 oz. Sunny's Goodtime Gator Green Glaze). Some flowers were painted with Sunny's Goodtime Apricot Colour Wash, and others were painted in pink, Benjamin Moore latex eggshell 2077-50, and yellow-gold, Benjamin Moore latex eggshell 348. The leaves and vines were done in green, Benjamin Moore latex eggshell 2029-30.

buckin' bronco
Pages 86–88: The wall basecoat is an off white with a yellow tint, Benjamin Moore Linen White Latex Eggshell. Below the border is Sunny's Goodtime Original Antique Aging Glaze. The actual border was painted in dark red, Benjamin Moore latex eggshell 1308. The boot stencil was done in a medium brown, Benjamin Moore latex eggshell 1132.

rugby stripe
Pages 89–91: The wall basecoat is a pale blue, Benjamin Moore latex eggshell 813. The wall finish is Sunny's Goodtime Marine Glaze. The green stripe was painted in Benjamin Moore latex eggshell 2029-30. Page 91: **Yellow colorwash with green stripe alternate:** The wall basecoat is a yellow-gold, Benjamin Moore latex eggshell 348. The 12" (30.5 cm) stripe is Sunny's Goodtime Apricot Colour Wash. The 1/4" (6 mm) stripe was done in green, Benjamin Moore latex eggshell 2029-30.

PART 4: ROOMS TO THINK AND DREAM IN (ages 9 through 12)

cotton candy stripes
Pages 94–96: The wall basecoat is Benjamin Moore latex eggshell White. The stripes were done in Sunny's Goodtime Bubblegum Pink Colour Wash combination color (mix 16 oz. Sunny's Goodtime Palm Beach Pink Colour Wash with 8 oz. Sunny's Goodtime Ruby Red Glaze). Page 96: **Pink walls with green stripe alternate:** The wall basecoat is a pale pink, Benjamin Moore latex eggshell 884. The 12" (30.5 cm) stripe was done in Sunny's Goodtime Bubblegum Pink Colour Wash combination color (mix 16 oz. Sunny's Goodtime Palm Beach Pink with 8 oz. Sunny's Goodtime Ruby Red Glaze). The 1/4" (6 mm) stripe was painted with an avocado green, Benjamin Moore latex eggshell 2029-50.

log cabin
Pages 97–99: The wall basecoat is an off-white with a yellow tint, Benjamin Moore latex eggshell Linen White. The log cabin pattern was created with Sunny's Goodtime Cappuccino Glaze.

mermaid's bower
Pages 100-103: The wall basecoat is Benjamin Moore latex eggshell White. The wash and swirl pattern was created with Sunny's Goodtime Marine Glaze and the dots with Benjamin Moore Spring Hill Green 412 latex eggshell.

sticks and stripes
Pages 104–106: The wall basecoat is a light khaki, Benjamin Moore latex eggshell 1044, as are the 2" (5 cm) and 6 " (15 cm) stripes. The 14" (35.6 cm) stripe was done in Sunny's Goodtime Original Antique Aging Glaze. The 1/4" (6 mm) and 2" (5 cm) stripes were done in a medium tan, Benjamin Moore latex eggshell HC-76. The 5 1/2" (14 cm) stripe was painted with Sunny's Goodtime Apricot Colour Wash and the 3" (7.5 cm) and 6" (15 cm) stripes with Sunny's Goodtime French Gray Colour Wash. The 1" (2.5 cm) stripe was painted with Sunny's Goodtime Fern Glaze combination color (Gator Green Glaze + Original Glaze) and the 3/4" (1.9 cm) stripe with Sunny's Goodtime Apricot Colour Wash. The 1/4" (6 mm) stripe was done in a medium purple, Benjamin Moore latex eggshell 1405.

catch a wave
Pages 107–110: The wall basecoat is a pale blue, Benjamin Moore latex eggshell 813. The paint below the wave border is Sunny's Goodtime Marine Glaze. Page 110: **White with light blue colorwash alternate:** The wall basecoat is Benjamin Moore latex eggshell White, washed with Sunny's Bahama Blue Colour Wash.

painted headboard
Pages 111–113: The wall basecoat is a pale yellow, Benjamin Moore latex eggshell 211. The headboard design was painted in a light blue, Benjamin Moore latex eggshell 815.

at home in the castle

Pages 114–118: The wall basecoat is an off-white with a yellow tint, Benjamin Moore latex eggshell Linen White. The stoneblock pattern is Sunny's Goodtime Original Antique Aging Glaze.

garden girl

Pages 119–121: The wall basecoat is a pale pink, Benjamin Moore latex eggshell 894. The vines are Sunny's Goodtime Grass Glaze combination color (mix 8 oz. Sunny's Goodtime Gator Green Glaze with 16 oz. Sunny's Goodtime Sunshine Daydream Glaze) and Sunny's Goodtime Avocado Colour Wash combination color (mix 12 oz. Sunny's Goodtime Lizard Lime Colour Wash with 12 oz. Sunny's Goodtime Gator Green Glaze). The flowers were painted in red-orange, Benjamin Moore latex eggshell 1306.

grandmother's house

Pages 123–124: The wall basecoat is an off-white with a yellow tint, Benjamin Moore latex eggshell Linen White. The wall finish is Sunny's Goodtime Bahama Blue Colour Wash. Page 124: **Yellow colorwash alternate:** The wall basecoat is an off-white with a yellow tint, Benjamin Moore latex eggshell Linen White. The walls were colorwashed with Sunny's Goodtime Sunshine Daydream Glaze. Page 124: **Pink colorwash alternate:** The wall basecoat is an off-white with a yellow tint, Benjamin Moore latex eggshell Linen White. The walls were colorwashed with Sunny's Goodtime Bubblegum Pink Colour Wash combination color (mix 16 oz. Sunny's Goodtime Palm Beach Pink Colour Wash with 8 oz. Sunny's Goodtime Ruby Red Glaze).

up, up and away!

Pages 125–128: The wall basecoat is a tan, Benjamin Moore latex eggshell 1047. The area below the border was done in Sunny's Goodtime Original Antique Aging Glaze. The actual rope border was painted in a medium yellow, Benjamin Moore latex eggshell 290, and a medium tan, Benjamin Moore latex eggshell 228. Page 127-129: **The custom chalkboard paint** is a mix of 32 oz. of a medium gray-brown, Benjamin Moore latex flat HC-69 with 16 oz. Sunny's Goodtime Clear Glaze and 8 oz. of unsanded tile grout. The chalkboard border tassels were painted in a dark red, Benjamin Moore latex eggshell 1309, and a brick red, Benjamin Moore latex eggshell 2008-10. Page 129: **Chalkboard alternate:** The wall basecoat is a pale pink, Benjamin Moore latex eggshell 884. The tent was painted in a medium purple-blue, Benjamin Moore latex eggshell 2067-50. The chalkboard was painted in black Crayola chalkboard paint.

knot knot

Pages 130–131: The wall basecoat is a light blue, Benjamin Moore latex eggshell 792. The sailing knot was painted in a light tan, Benjamin Moore latex eggshell HC-80, and in Benjamin Moore latex eggshell White.

Sunny's Colour Washes and Glazes

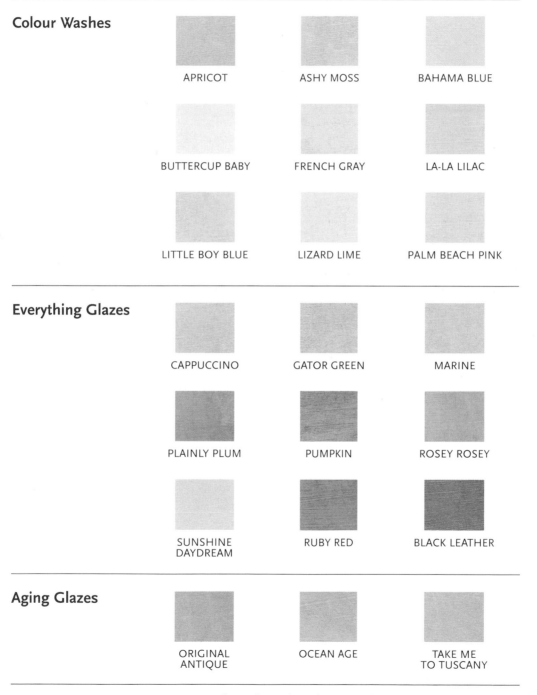

Colour Washes

APRICOT   ASHY MOSS   BAHAMA BLUE

BUTTERCUP BABY   FRENCH GRAY   LA-LA LILAC

LITTLE BOY BLUE   LIZARD LIME   PALM BEACH PINK

Everything Glazes

CAPPUCCINO   GATOR GREEN   MARINE

PLAINLY PLUM   PUMPKIN   ROSEY ROSEY

SUNSHINE DAYDREAM   RUBY RED   BLACK LEATHER

Aging Glazes

ORIGINAL ANTIQUE   OCEAN AGE   TAKE ME TO TUSCANY

NOTE: Colors will vary depending on application and basecoat color.

Visit sunnysgoodtimepaint.com on the Internet for more information.

index